Instructor's Manual and Test Bank

for

Assessment of Exceptional Students: Educational and Psychological Procedures

Fifth Edition

Instructor's Manual and Test Bank

for

Assessment of Exceptional Students: Educational and Psychological Procedures

Fifth Edition

Prepared by

Ronald L. Taylor
Florida Atlantic University

Allyn and Bacon
Boston   London   Toronto   Sydney   Tokyo   Singapore

TABLE OF CONTENTS

PREFACE

OVERVIEW OF THE TEXT

Assessment of Exceptional Students: Educational and Psychological Procedures (5th Ed.) was designed for use by students preparing to be special education teachers, diagnosticians, specialists, school psychologists and general education teachers. It is also extremely relevant for teachers/practitioners who are already working with exceptional children.

In general, the use of the text will depend on the experience and background of the students. For example, graduate students might be encouraged to focus on the research sections of the chapters. This could involve an analysis and critique of primary sources. Most chapters in the text contain information that is relevant for all exceptional children. Chapter 17 is relevant for children from birth to age five with disabilities whereas Chapter 18 is designed to be about adolescents and young adults with special needs. There are several unique features of this textbook that give the instructor flexibility while offering a cohesive structure for the student. These include:

1) the emphasis on a pragmatic approach to assessment;

2) a summary matrix presented at the end of each chapter that includes a discussion of the instruments/techniques. This matrix allows for comparison of the instruments regarding **suggested use** and **target population** as well as including any **special considerations** that users need to know. Finally, the **educational relevance for exceptional students** is given for each instrument/technique. The matrices are directly related to the assessment model presented in Chapter 2;

3) the inclusion of both informal and formal assessment procedures, emphasizing how each fits into the assessment process;

4) a thorough review of relevant research for each norm-referenced instrument. This aspect emphasizes the use of the test with exceptional students;

5) an overview section for each norm-referenced test. This section includes the age range, technical adequacy, and suggested use, making this text a valuable reference tool;

6) the inclusion of instruments/techniques for both individuals

with mild/moderate disabilities and those with severe/profound disabilities. The examples in the last chapter reflect this emphasis;

7) the use of vignettes to introduce the chapters that focus on ability and achievement tests. These vignettes indicate the typical use of certain types of tests. The instructor should point out if and why these uses are inappropriate.

FORMAT OF INSTRUCTORS MANUAL

This Instructors Manual is designed to be used with **Assessment of Exceptional Students: Educational and Psychological Procedures** (5th Ed.). For each chapter in the text, this manual provides the following:

1) <u>Overview and Teaching Suggestions</u> - this section summarizes the content of each chapter and indicates the specific issues/topics that should be emphasized (for those chapters in which instruments/techniques are included, the instructor should decide which ones to emphasize in the lectures). Note: whenever possible, the tests discussed should be brought to class and made available for student inspection.

2) <u>Activities</u> - this section provides specific suggestions for in-class and out-of-class learning activities. A description, rationale, and statement of expected student outcome are included.

3) <u>Test Questions</u> - included in this section are approximately 35 test items (including multiple choice and true-false) for each chapter. In all, over 650 items are available. The page number in the text where the answer to each question can be found is presented at the end of each chapter. In addition, open-ended questions are provided that also may be used for class discussion items or study purposes.

4) <u>Exhibits</u> - for many of the proposed activities, materials are needed. The exhibits that are included in this section correspond to the various activities. For example, in chapter 11, exhibit 11-2 corresponds to activity 11-2. The exhibits are presented on separate pages to facilitate reproduction for student use. The correct answers to exhibits are given in the activities section.

Chapter 1

Assessment: Historical, Philosophical, and Legal Considerations

OVERVIEW AND TEACHING SUGGESTIONS

In this chapter, the historical, philosophical, and legal events that have played an important role in shaping assessment policies and procedures currently used in schools were discussed. From an historical perspective, the interest in standardized assessment in the areas of intelligence, personality, and achievement developed in the first half of the twentieth century. As special education emerged as a formal field in the 1960s, interest in standardized testing, particularly for students with learning disabilities, increased. By the 1970s, however, standardized testing was viewed negatively due to issues such as the overreliance on perceptual-motor testing, discriminatory assessment practices, and the prominence of the behavioral model. In the mid 1980s, the Regular Education Initiative impacted assessment practices by emphasizing informal assessment as part of prereferral intervention. In the 1990s, the concept of full inclusion resulted in the general education teacher assuming additional assessment responsibilities.

Both litigation and legislation have affected assessment procedures. Issues regarding the discriminatory uses of tests and the timely delivery of assessment procedures have resulted in landmark cases. Many notable court cases were reviewed in this chapter. Significant legislation included in this chapter are PL 94-142, PL 99-457, PL 101-476 (IDEA), the Americans with Disabilities Act (ADA) and PL 105-17, the latest reauthorization of IDEA. The following topics should be emphasized in this chapter.

*standardized testing in the early 20th century

*process testing in the 1960s

*the Regular Education Initiative

*full inclusion

*assessment litigation cases

*impact of the following federal legislation on assessment

   practices:

   PL 94-142

   PL 99-457

   PL 101-476

   ADA

   PL 105-17

ACTIVITIES

1-1 UNDERSTANDING FULL INCLUSION

Purpose - To focus students' attention on the major tenets of the full inclusion movement.
Description - After a class discussion concerning full inclusion, ask students to prepare (as a take-home assignment) a speech to the local school board that would explain how full inclusion might be implemented in the public school system. Focus should be on the way in which inclusion might affect current assessment procedures.

Half the students should be assigned the "con" position, while the other half should be given the "pro" position. A sampling of the prepared speeches can be presented at a subsequent class.

1-2 IMPACT OF THE LARRY P. DECISION

Purpose - To determine the impact that a court case can have on the assessment practices of a state.
Description - Have the students locate and read articles that investigate the effects that the Larry P. decision had on the assessment procedures in the state of California. Students should be encouraged to discuss this issue focusing on areas such as the effects of declassification. Examples of relevant references are:

Bersoff, D. (1980). Larry P. v. Riles: Legal perspective. School Psychology Review, 2, 112-122.

Forness, S. (1985). Effects of public policy at the state level: California's impact on MR, LD, and ED categories. Remedial and Special Education, 6, 36-43.

MacMillan, D., & Balow, I. (1991). Impact of Larry P. on educational programs and assessment practices in California. Diagnostique, 17, 57-69.

MacMillan, D., Hendrick, I., & Watkins, A. (1988). Impact of Diana, Larry P. and PL 94-142 on minority students. Exceptional Children, 54, 426-432.

Taylor, R. (1997). Nondiscriminatory evaluation. In R. Taylor (Ed.) Assessment of individuals with mental retardation. (pps. 55-72).San Diego:Singular Publishing Group.

Turnbull, R. (1993). Free and appropriate education (3rd ed.). Denver: Love Publishing Co.

MULTIPLE CHOICE QUESTIONS

1. Prior to the emergence of the field of special education, most assessment issues were related to the measurement of
   a) physical health
  *b) intelligence and personality
   c) psychological processing
   d) reading and math

2. From the 1920s - 1950s, a variety of assessment instruments used to measure personality and emotional status were tied to the field of
   a) medicine
   b) special education
   *c) psychology
   d) general education

3. As a result of the application of the medical/neurological model during the 1960s _____ became very popular.
   a) intelligence testing
   *b) process testing
   c) personality testing
   d) functional testing

4. The belief that perceptual motor skills would generalize to academic areas led to
   *a) the use of perceptual-motor tests to predict achievement
   b) the use of perceptual-motor tests to predict intelligence
   c) the development of remedial programs specifically designed for academic skills
   d) professionals stressing academic skills development

5. The evidence for the effectiveness of perceptual-motor training indicates that
   a) academic ability improves with training
   b) cognitive ability improves with training
   *c) academic ability does not improve with training
   d) both a and b

6. The role of the special educator in a full inclusion setting is to
   a) work with the special education students in that setting
   b) team teach with the general education teacher
   c) work as a consultant for the general education teacher
   *d) all of the above

7. The Regular Education Initiative (REI) called for
   a) the use of standardized testing before referral
   *b) prereferral assessment and intervention
   c) an increase in the number of students labeled
   d) none of the above

8. The first major court case focusing on the misuse or discriminatory use of test information was
   a) Guadalupe vs. Tempe
   b) Larry P. vs. Riles
   *c) Hobson vs. Hanson
   d) Diana vs. State Board of Education

9. The case that established that there should be assessment of
   primary language competence was
   a) PASE vs. Hannon
   *b) Diana vs. State Board of Education
   c) Hobson vs. Hanson
   d) Larry P. vs. Riles

10. Which case resulted in the complete prohibition of using
    intelligence tests with African-American students for the
    purpose of identification or placement into special education?
    *a) Larry P. vs. Riles
    b) PASE vs. Hannon
    c) Hobson vs. Hanson
    d) Crawford vs. Honig

11. Nondiscriminatory evaluation was first mandated by
    a) Public Law 99-457
    b) Public Law 101-476
    *c) Public Law 94-142
    d) Public Law 105-17

12. Emphasis on alternate assessment and functional behavior
    assessment was primarily the result of
    a) Public Law 94-142
    b) Public Law 99-457
    c) Public Law 101-476
    *d) Public Law 105-17

13. Parental participation as mandated by PL 105-17 impacts
    assessment by allowing parents to
    a) examine all records
    b) refuse evaluation of their child
    c) have an independent evaluation of their child
    *d) all of the above

14. Public Law 99-457 has created a need for more and improved
    diagnostic procedures for
    a) adolescents and young adults
    *b) children birth through age 5
    c) students with vocational needs
    d) children three through age 8

15. One of the effects of Public Law 101-476 on assessment is in
    the area of
    a) preschool evaluation
    b) early intervention
    *c) transitional/vocational evaluation
    d) informal evaluation

16. In which case did the judge conclude that intelligence test bias had an insignificant influence on psychoeducational assessment?
   *a) PASE vs. Hannon
   b) Crawford vs. Honig
   c) Larry P vs. Riles
   d) Hobson vs. Hanson

17. One of the conclusions reached by the court in Jose P vs. Ambach was that
   a) the district must provide prereferral intervention before a student was referred
   b) the district must provide appropriate intervention after a student was referred
   *c) the district must provide a timely evaluation after a student was referred
   d) the district must provide a prereferral evaluation before a student was referred

18. The first formal attempt of providing an objective measure of intelligence was the
   a) Rorschach Ink Blot Test
   b) Thematic Apperception Test
   c) Terman-Binet
   *d) Stanford-Binet

TRUE-FALSE QUESTIONS

19. Alfred Binet perhaps had the first major impact on the use of assessment instruments with exceptional individuals. T

20. Thematic picture tests and personality inventories are still used today because their relevance in education has been questioned. T

21. Research supports the fact that most general education teachers feel that they have adequate training to teach special education students in an inclusive setting. F

22. "Process testing", although popular in the 1960s lost its popularity in the 1970s. T

23. Perceptual-motor tests can successfully determine modality preference for academic learning. F

24. Perceptual-motor training was an effective intervention technique for improving academic, cognitive, and perceptual-motor skills. F

25. PL 94-142's requirement of an Individualized Education Program included the identification of goals but not objectives. F

26. If parents have a private evaluation for their child before the school district conducts theirs, the parents are responsible for the cost. T

27. In the Gerstmeyer v. Howard Public Schools case, the Court required the district to reimburse the costs of private schooling and tutoring because of the delay in evaluation services for a child. T

28. The nondiscriminatory evaluation clause of PL 94-142 was retained in concept in PL 105-17. T

29. In Luke S. and Hans S. vs. Nix et al, the court ruled that the state should provide more prereferral assessment. T

30. According to PL 105-17, a full reevaluation of a child receiving special education services is required every three years. F

31. Among the recommendations of PL 99-457 was the need to identify and establish programs for infants and toddlers with disabilities. T

32. Transitional services that includes vocational evaluation was one emphasis of PL 101-476. T

33. In Hobson v. Hanson, the importance of evaluating adaptive behavior before labeling a student as having mental retardation was noted. T

34. Both IDEA and ADA provide assurances for individuals with disabilities throughout the lifespan. F

35. Litigation based on the Larry P. case continued in the Crawford v. Honig case. T

OPEN-ENDED OR DISCUSSION QUESTIONS

36. Compare and contrast the Larry P. vs. Riles and the PASE vs. Hannon court cases.

37. Assume that you are the assessment specialist in your school and you are speaking with parents of a child referred for special education. Explain both the parent's and the student's rights during the assessment process.

Chapter 2

The Assessment Process:
A Proposed Model

OVERVIEW AND TEACHING SUGGESTIONS

This chapter provides a general introduction to the area of assessment. Six prerequisite questions that must be addressed prior to initiating an assessment are discussed along with possible answers: (1) Why assess? (2) How is the process initiated? (3) What procedures should you use? (4) When should you assess? (5) Who should assess? and (6) What should you do with the results? These prerequisite questions serve as a basis for an assessment model. The assessment model presented in this chapter includes both a prereferral and postreferral component and focuses on a pragmatic approach that emphasizes the purpose for a given assessment. The following topics should be emphasized:

*the importance of prerequisite questions

*various purposes of assessment

*types of tests (including advantages and disadvantages)

*types of scores yielded by norm-referenced tests

*other types of assessment data that can be collected

*distinction between formal and informal assessment

*importance of prereferral assessment

ACTIVITIES

2-1 INTRODUCTION TO ASSESSMENT: A CASE STUDY
Purpose - To provide the student with an opportunity to respond to

a case study relative to the assessment issues presented in this chapter.

Description - This activity can be done as an in-class group discussion or a take-home assignment. Provide students with a brief case study of a second grade child who is having difficulty in mathematics (Exhibit 2-1). Present the following questions: (1) should an assessment be conducted? (2) who should conduct the assessment? (3) in general, what type of assessment techniques should be used? and (4) when should this assessment be conducted?

MULTIPLE CHOICE QUESTIONS

38. A test that measures "how much" someone knows in a particular area without time limits, is
   *a) a power test
   b) a criterion-referenced test
   c) a standardized test
   d) a norm-referenced test

39. One possible use of screening tests is to
   a) provide a comprehensive evaluation relative to the educational and social/psychological status of the individual
   b) determine specific causes for a suspected learning disability
   *c) identify "high risk" individuals who may experience difficulties at a later date
   d) identify specific goals and objectives

40. If, as a teacher, you were interested in how a student compared to a standardization sample at his grade level in arithmetic and you also wanted to observe how he approached the tasks you would probably choose a(n)
   a) group norm-referenced arithmetic test
   *b) individual norm-referenced arithmetic test
   c) individual criterion-referenced arithmetic test
   d) group or individual criterion-referenced arithmetic test

41. Not all children are identified using educational and psychological tests. For example students with _____ are frequently identified using other procedures.
   a) learning disabilities
   *b) orthopedic disabilities
   c) mild mental retardation
   d) behavior disorders

42. A derived score
    a) is the same as a standard deviation
    b) is yielded from a criterion-referenced test
   *c) allows for the interpretation of a raw score from a norm-referenced test
    d) always has a mean of 100

43. If a test yields a standard score with a mean of 50 and a standard deviation of 10 and is administered to a random sample of 1000 students, approximately how many individuals will score between 40 and 60?
    a) 340   c) 990
   *b) 680   d) 1000

44. An Individualized Education Program must include
    a) standardized test results
   *b) information on how the disability affects involvement in the general education curriculum
    c) information regarding a student's sociocultural background
    d) criterion-referenced test results

45. Which statement is true concerning the prereferral and postreferral components of the assessment model?
    a) the prereferral is the most important
    b) the postreferral is the most important
   *c) both components serve a purpose although the prereferral should usually be implemented first
    d) both components serve a purpose although the postreferral should usually be initiated first

46. In educational and psychological norm-referenced testing, the norms are established by
   *a) administering the test to a standardization sample
    b) controlled experiments
    c) application of personality theory
    d) consensus of experts

47. Criterion-referenced tests
   *a) measure a student's mastery of certain skills
    b) compare students to national norms
    c) are similar to norm-referenced approaches
    d) emphasize differences between students

48. Regarding the referral process,
    a) documentation of the suspected problem is only necessary in severe cases
    *b) preliminary assessment data should be collected
    c) a student should be referred as soon as a problem is suspected
    d) all schools follow the same procedures

49. A grade equivalent (e.g., 4.1) indicates a student's performance relative to
    a) placement within a curriculum
    *b) students in the same grade in the standardization sample
    c) the age of the student
    d) the IQ of the student

50. Normal curve equivalents can be viewed as
    a) a combination of raw scores and percentile ranks
    b) a type of standard score
    *c) a combination of standard scores and percentile ranks
    d) a type of percentile rank

51. PRO-SCORE
    a) is a hand-scoring method that prevents errors
    *b) is a computer program for scoring norm-referenced tests
    c) provides only derived scores
    d) can be used to score any test

52. In general, group tests
    a) should be used for program placement
    b) are usually used for diagnostic purposes
    c) permit observation of a student's approach to a task
    *d) are usually used for screening purposes

53. An assessment procedure in which the child is not actively involved is
    a) observation
    b) curriculum-based assessment
    *c) analysis of the home environment
    d) portfolio assessment

54. Which of the following is an example of formal assessment?
    *a) norm-referenced tests
    b) observation
    c) error analyses
    d) analysis of work products

TRUE-FALSE QUESTIONS

55. When a psychologist conducts an evaluation on a child referred for special education services it is important for the child's teacher to be involved in the assessment. T

56. Curriculum-based assessment stresses evaluation for instructional planning rather than for labeling purposes. T

57. When a child starts to demonstrate some type of mild learning problem, it is best to refer the child immediately for a comprehensive, multidisciplinary evaluation. F

58. A statement addressing transition service needs is required for all students, regardless of age. F

59. Special education students are exempt from participating in state-wide or district-wide assessment programs. F

60. Norm-referenced rather than criterion-referenced tests are administered for labeling and classification purposes. T

61. Group administered tests are preferable to individually administered tests for diagnostic and program placement decisions. F

62. The International Reading Association recommend the use of grade equivalents because they are the easiest for teachers to interpret. F

63. A popular trend in assessment is to evaluate entire classes of students using tests based on the curriculum being used. T

64. The purpose for assessment is not important in determining who conducts the assessment. F

65. The intent of portfolio assessment is to focus on both the process and the product of learning. T

66. Tests are simply devices to which individuals are exposed that give a qualitative or subjective characterization of one or more traits of those individuals. F

67. Research has shown that if a student is referred for special education, there is a good chance that he/she will be found eligible. T

13

68. It is important to determine the task requirements of a test in order to interpret results. T

69. Many of the tests used in special education are a combination of power and speed. T

70. Results from specific assessment procedures can often be used for more than one purpose.

71. Criteria used to determine special education labels can differ from state to state. T

72. Portfolios are helpful because they can demonstrate both the depth and breadth of a student's work. T

OPEN-ENDED QUESTIONS OR DISCUSSION TOPICS

73. What are the relative strengths and weaknesses of norm-referenced and criterion-referenced measures?

74. Delineate the advantages and disadvantages of group versus individual tests.

Item #	Page #	Item #	Page #
38.	38	56.	38
39.	24	57.	45
40.	39	58.	28
41.	26	59.	28
42.	33	60.	46
43.	35	61.	39
44.	28	62.	34
45.	46	63.	38
46.	33	64.	23
47.	37	65.	41
48.	24	66.	32
49.	33	67.	32
50.	36	68.	37
51.	37	69.	38
52.	39	70.	23
53.	39	71.	26
54.	41	72.	41
55.	42		

Exhibit 2-1

Case Study: Assessment Issues

A second grade teacher observes that one of his students is falling behind his other students in the area of arithmetic. Because it is early in the school year, the teacher has not determined what is causing the problem or how far behind the student actually is. His concern is based on the student's poor performance on weekly in-class tests and on worksheets.

Chapter 3

Practical Considerations

OVERVIEW AND TEACHING SUGGESTIONS

There are several major factors to consider during the assessment process. These factors pertain specifically to formal assessment procedures although they have relevance as guidelines for informal procedures as well. All of these factors should be considered throughout the assessment process. Acknowledgment of them will help in attempting to reduce some of the error involved in assessment and will aid in putting the information in its proper perspective.

The first factor relates to the examinee or the person being tested. Included in this category are such issues as anxiety and motivation, test wiseness, health and emotional status, type of disability and attitudes of the person being tested. All of these can affect test performance.

The second major factor focuses on the examiner. Test administration and interpretation differences, styles of interacting with the examinee, bias, racial/cultural differences of the examiner and examinee, and errors made scoring were discussed in this category.

The last major factor is related to the test itself, including its validity and reliability. Various methods to determine validity and reliability were reviewed. Other characteristics of the test that should be considered are the standard error of measurement, the population used to standardize a norm-referenced test, and the rationale and use of Baals and ceilings. Possible test bias is also an important and controversial consideration.

The following points should be highlighted in this chapter:

   *specific factors related to the examinee that can affect assessment results

   *the relatively high frequency of administration and scoring errors

   *examiner-examinee differences and their relative effect on test performance

   *thorough understanding of the importance of reliability and validity

   *how to interpret reliability and validity coefficients

   *relevance of the SEM

   *various types of bias

ACTIVITIES

3-1 REVIEW AND DISCUSSION OF CONTENT VALIDITY

Purpose - To provide students with an opportunity to review a spelling test and to evaluate the content validity.
Description - provide students with a general spelling test (Exhibit 3-1) that purportedly measures an individual's overall spelling ability. The test was intentionally developed to have poor content validity and other shortcomings that make it ineffective for the intended use. Divide the class into small groups and instruct each group to identify the test's strengths and weaknesses. After 15 minutes, each group should present their conclusions.
   Emphasis should be placed on the test's limited number of items and the unrepresentative sampling of words. The groups can also develop a more representative, appropriate instrument as an additional exercise.

3-2 CULTURALLY FAIR ASSESSMENTS

Purpose - To help students understand the difficulty of developing a culturally fair assessment.

Description - As a take-home assignment, have students analyze instruments that purport to be culturally fair (e.g., the Cattell, the SOMPA, the K-ABC, etc.) and determine the method used to make them unbiased. Students should present their findings at a subsequent class meeting, with discussion concerning the merits and problems involved with the particular tests that they researched.

MULTIPLE CHOICE QUESTIONS

75. A correlation coefficient
    *a) ranges from -1 to +1
     b) is a derived score
     c) measures the amount of variance
     d) is expressed as an F-ratio

76. In general, validity refers to whether a test is
     a) consistent
     b) comprehensive
    *c) measuring what it purports to measure
     d) sufficiently detailed

77. In addition to the magnitude of the correlation coefficient, the _____ is important in interpreting the criterion-related validity of a test.
     a) standard deviation
    *b) validity of the criterion measure
     c) standard error of measurement
     d) number of items

78. The two types of criterion-related validity are
     a) retrospective & predictive
     b) concurrent & content
     c) content & construct
    *d) concurrent & predictive

79. The extent to which a test measures a theoretical construct or trait is called
     a) regression to the mean
     b) variability
    *c) construct validity
     d) test-retest reliability

80. The split-half procedure is
    *a) a way of establishing a test's internal reliability
    b) an interscorer test of reliability
    c) used to establish a test's validity
    d) none of the above

81. Which of the following is not a type of test reliability?
    *a) construct
    b) alternate form
    c) test-retest
    d) split-half

82. The point in a test at which the examiner assumes that all, earlier items would be answered correctly is called the
    *a) basal
    b) floor
    c) ceiling
    d) zenith

83. Which one of the following is a type of bias?
    a) factor analytic bias   c) item bias
    b) psychometric bias   *d) all of the above

84. Administering a test to a group of students and then readministering the same test to the same group two weeks later is a way of determining
    a) split-half reliability
    b) concurrent validity
    *c) test-retest reliability
    d) predictive validity

85. Which of the following is not a factor related to the examinee that might affect test results?
    a) health and emotional state
    b) test wiseness
    c) anxiety
    d) all of the above are factors

86. Which of the following does not need to be considered in order to establish content validity?
    a) appropriate testing methods
    b) appropriate test items
    c) completeness of the item sample
    *d) age of the student

87. Construct validity is established
    a) through careful construction of test items
    b) through completeness of a construct sample
   *c) through careful empirical studies
    d) through administration of a similar test

88. Which of the following is the most commonly used method to
    determine reliability?
   *a) test-retest
    b) test-retest with alternate forms
    c) equivalent-form
    d) criterion-related

89. Some argue that the best method to establish reliability is
    through
    a) interrater reliability
    b) equivalent-form reliability
    c) internal reliability
   *d) test-retest with alternate form reliability

90. The standard error of measurement
    a) is related to validity
   *b) provides a range that more accurately reflects how a
       person's score approaches their true score
    c) is higher when you can be more confident the score is an
       estimation of a true score
    d) is relatively unimportant to test interpretation

91. Item bias occurs when
    a) individuals have been taught specific test items
   *b) specific items are considered to be outside the life
       experiences of certain individuals
    c) items grouped together correlate highly with one another,
       but have low correlations with other groups
    d) an individual consistently misses the same items of a test

92. The most common definition of test bias is
   *a) mean difference bias
    b) psychometric bias
    c) factor-analytic bias
    d) item bias

TRUE-FALSE QUESTIONS

93. Reinforcement has not really been shown to affect test
    performance F

20

94. In general, research has indicated that African-American children will score lower on tests if examiners of a different ethnic group administer them. F

95. Because norm-referenced tests are administered in a standardized fashion, scoring errors are not a concern to the evaluator. F

96. Interscorer or interrater reliability is concerned with how two people score a test or rate a behavior. T

97. The term "norm" refers to "normal" when considering the nature of a standardization sample. F

98. Because "test-wiseness" can affect a student's performance on a test, it is advisable to provide instruction in test-taking skills. T

99. Test performance in certain areas can be improved by practicing test taking skills. T

100. Information about a student (e.g., race, gender) will not affect an examiner's scoring and interpretation of tests. F

101. Stress behaviors during testing have been noted in children as early as kindergarten age. T

102. In deciding whether or not to use certain types of reinforcers with examinees, the age of the student is an important consideration. T

103. Research has indicated reducing test anxiety results in improvement in test performance. F

104. The basal of a test is always three in a row correct. F

105. Examiner bias is not necessarily a conscious act. T

106. Some research indicates that familiarity with the examiner will affect the test performance of Hispanic and African-American children. T

107. The tendency to make scoring error appears to begin early in a professional's career. T

108. If a test is reliable, by definition it is valid. F

109. The ceiling of a test is the point at which the examiner assumes that the student could answer easier items. F

OPEN-ENDED QUESTIONS AND DISCUSSION TOPICS

110. What examinee factors can influence the results of an assessment?

111. If an examiner has prior knowledge of previous test results of an examine, can this knowledge influence the examiner's administration and interpretation of a standardized test? If so, how?

112. What is meant by nondiscriminatory evaluation? What steps can be used to try and ensure that an evaluation will be nondiscriminatory?

Exhibit 3-1

I. cat

2. arm

3. resilient

4. assiduous

5. acquiesce

6. pusillanimous

7. iridescence

8. sovereignty

9. medieval

10. loquacious

Instruction: State to the examinee: "This is a spelling test. After I say the word, please print the correct spelling"

Intended use: This spelling test was designed to measure an individual's overall spelling skills and to provide a standard score, percentile rank, and grade equivalent for students from kindergarten through grade 12.

Chapter 4

Observational Assessment

OVERVIEW AND TEACHING STRATEGIES

Observation is perhaps the most widely used method of assessing students. It is therefore important to use a systematic approach when observing a student's behavior. This involves the careful identification of target behaviors and the accurate recording of data.

Observation can be either informal or formal. The informal systems include observation when the observer is already present in the natural environment, when there is an external or outside observer in the natural setting, and when the observer is not present in the actual natural setting. Advantages and disadvantages of each were discussed. The formal systems include coding or notational procedures that allow for greater communication between observers. In addition, the more formal systems consider behavioral interactions rather than the behavior of a single student.

In addition to observing student behavior, assessment of the instructional environment is a source of pertinent information. The utility and procedures for this source were also reviewed. Moreover, recording procedures and recording devices were discussed that are essential to systematic observation.

Observation can be used initially to identify students in need of further assessment or to evaluate the effectiveness of various teaching/intervention approaches. In other words, it is a crucial aspect of both the prereferral and postreferral components of the assessment model.

Observation can also be used as a crucial component in conducting a <u>functional behavior assessment(FBA)</u>. FBA is used to determine the intent or purpose of a student's behavior. It is required if the school district changes a student's placement due to maladaptive behavior.

The following specific topics should be emphasized in this chapter.

*emphasis on assessing in the "natural" environment

*issue of reactivity

*importance of precise identification of target behavior

*the need for objective data collection procedures

*types of behaviors for which the various recording procedures are relevant

*importance of collecting baseline data

*advantages and disadvantages of the various formal observation packages

*observation of the instructional environment

*steps in conducting a functional behavior assessment

<u>ACTIVITIES</u>

4-1 IDENTIFYING AND RECORDING TARGET BEHAVIORS

<u>Purpose</u> - To give the students experience in the area of observational assessment. Specifically this activity demonstrates the importance of operational definitions of target behaviors and

gives the student a chance to choose the most appropriate recording procedure.

Description - Choose a videotape of a student with a mild disability in a classroom setting. The videotape should be about 10 minutes long and should show the student engaging in a variety of activities. Have students (in small groups) (1) observe the student and identify a target behavior, (2) choose the most appropriate recording procedure, (3) observe the student again and record the behaviors, (4) compare their data, and (6) discuss any discrepancies. A general discussion of the importance of being specific in the identification of the target behavior can follow. The tape may be shown again to see if the reliability of the observations increase after the discussion.

4-2 OBSERVATIONS IN NATURAL VERSUS ACADEMIC SETTINGS

Purpose - To highlight the differences in behavior that may be apparent when a student is observed in a natural versus a classroom setting.

Description - Have students observe a student with learning problems in both the classroom as well as the playground, lunchroom, or home environment. Students should first target specific behaviors to record, then as unobtrusively as possible record the student's behaviors in both settings chosen. Written reports should be discussed in a subsequent class to highlight the importance of observing student behavior in a variety of settings before coming to definite conclusions regarding academic and social programming.

MULTIPLE CHOICE QUESTIONS

113. Ms. Harler is interested in the number of math problems one of her students, Cindy, can complete during a ten-minute period. She decided to use a(n) _____ recording procedure to collect baseline data.
    *a) event (frequency)   c) latency
    b) duration   d) interval

114. After his teacher tells him to erase the board, Phillip invariably spends several minutes avoiding the task. His teacher felt that _____ recording would be the most appropriate procedure to use.
    a) event (frequency)   *c) latency
    b) duration   d) interval

115. Careful identification of a target behavior requires that
    a) the behavior fall into some identifiable class
    b) the behavior be considered problematic
    *c) the behavior be precise, observable, and measurable
    d) the behavior be noted by a number of persons

116. Observation of student behaviors can be used for
    a) determining entry levels in specific areas of functioning
    b) early detection of learning problems
    c) making instructional decisions
    *d) all of the above

117. An advantage of formal observation systems is that they
    *a) facilitate communication among observers
    b) are simple to use
    c) are less time consuming than informal systems
    d) do not require -comprehensive observer training

118. One advantage of an informal observation in which the observer
    is already present in the environment is
    a) it is not difficult to find and manage the time
    *b) reactivity is not a serious issue
    c) it is more reliable than other types of observation
    d) it is more culture-fair

119. One variable that is not an important component in the
    assessment of a student's instructional environment is
    a) management and teaching procedures
    b) teacher behaviors
    *c) student distractibility
    d) space and objects in the environment

120. Collecting "baseline data" refers to
    a) noting changes in behavior after a specific intervention
    *b) observation/recording of behavior prior to an intervention
    c) determining an average frequency of behavior throughout
       the intervention
    d) determining the gain or loss of the target behavior
       following an intervention

121. The Standard Behavior Chart is used in
    *a) precision teaching
    b) norm-referenced tests
    c) power tests
    d) momentary time sampling procedures

122. Among other purposes, data from observational assessment can
     be used to
     a) "classify" students
     b) determine eligibility for special education
     c) make placement decisions
     *d) evaluate the effectiveness of a specific teaching program

123. Which of the following statement about functional behavior
     assessment is <u>false?</u>
     a) must be conducted when a student's educational placement
        is changed because of maladaptive behavior
     *b) is a new technique that requires special training
     c) can involve a variety of assessment techniques
     d) determines the purpose or intent of a behavior

124. One factor not important for designing an intervention program
     using an observational assessment model is
     a) precise and appropriate measurement of the target behavior
     b) systematic introduction of the intervention program
     *c) an in-depth explanation of the procedures to the student
        being observed
     d) evaluating the effectiveness of the program

125. The environmental variables that occur immediately prior to a
     behavior are referred to as
     *a) antecedents
     b) consequences
     c) baseline data
     d) replacement behaviors

126. For maximum reliability of observation sessions,
     a) utilize both informal and formal procedures
     b) use some type of subjective system
     *c) interrater agreement should be reached
     d) observe in the environment in which the problem occurs

127. Observer drift occurs when
     a) interrater reliability is low
     *b) the observer gradually shifts from the initial definition
        of the target behavior
     c) the observer gradually misses the opportunity to record
        data
     d) one observer replaces another

128. Which is not a device for counting behaviors?
     a) wrist counters
     b) abacus beads
     c) pencil and paper techniques
     *d) stop watches

129. Event recording involves
    *a) counting the occurrences of the target behavior
    b) observing the time and place the behavior occurred
    c) only the length of time the target behavior occurred
    d) behaviors that occur for long periods of time

130. A functional behavior manipulation is used when
    a) a behavior occurs in only one setting
    b) a behavior occurs at a very high rate
    *c) a consistent pattern of behavior cannot be determined
    d) an intervention program has been successful

131. The Manual for Coding Discrete Behaviors in the School Setting
    a) entails observation of the target child and his/her peers
    b) utilizes a coding system for behavior interactions
    c) was developed exclusively for the school environment
    *d) all of the above

132. The Instructional Environment Scale-2 (TIES-2) is a set of observation and interview forms that are used with
    a) teachers and students
    b) parents and students
    *c) teachers and parents
    d) teachers and principals

TRUE-FALSE QUESTIONS

133. As a general rule, observation requires more inference on the evaluator's part than other types of assessment. F

134. Reliability and validity are not important issues in observational assessment because no test scores are obtained.   F

135. Formal observational procedures typically include coding systems to record behavioral interactions. T

136. The Instructional Environment Scale-2 can best be described as a comprehensive assessment of a student's maladaptive behavior. F

137. A functional behavior analysis leads to a hypothesis about the possible function or purpose that a behavior serves. T

138. The Standard Behavior Chart is an instrument used in the Ecological Assessment of Child Problem Behavior. F

139. Informal observational approaches are more commonly used than formal systems. T

140. "Reactivity" occurs most often when the observer is already present in the environment. F

141. Before beginning an observational assessment, both the recording devices and the recording procedures should be identified. T

142. You cannot observe more than one child at a time if momentary time sampling is being used. F

143. Observation conducted by the observer already present in the natural environment is the most widely used informal procedure. T

144. Making decisions about entry behaviors is similar to determining the desired goal. F

145. A graph is a visual representation of observed behaviors. T

146. Event recording is best used when the behavior occurs at an extremely high frequency. F

147. When using the Manual for Coding Discrete Behaviors in the School Setting, only the behaviors of the target child are considered. F

OPEN ENDED QUESTIONS AND DISCUSSION TOPICS

148. Describe the steps in conducting a functional behavior assessment, giving an example of each step.

149. What are the advantages and disadvantages of the various types of recording procedures?

Item #	Page #	Item #	Page #
113.	72	131.	78
114.	74	132.	80
115.	68	133.	65
116.	66-67	134.	67
117.	78	135.	78
118.	66	136.	80
119.	80	137.	84
120.	69	138.	70
121.	70	139.	66
122.	77	140.	66
123.	81	141.	69
124.	68	142.	76

125.	82	143.	66
126.	67	144.	67
127.	69	145.	70
128.	69,70	146.	72
129.	72	147.	78
130.	85		

Chapter 5

Criterion-Referenced Testing
and Error Analysis

OVERVIEW

Criterion-referenced tests (CRTS) are an alternative to traditional assessment instruments. CRTs measure a limited domain with numerous items per area. They are designed so that the items will describe a student's performance on specific learning tasks. As such, CRTs provide information that can serve as the basis for the development of specific instructional programs. In other words, they provide information about what to teach; they also can be constructed to provide information about how to teach as well. Many have been developed and published commercially, whereas others are prepared by teachers/diagnosticians. This chapter discussed the principles and procedures that are utilized in the development of CRTS. It is important that CRTs be developed in a systematic and meaningful way.

Also discussed in this chapter was error analysis, which provides information about the process or strategies a student uses to complete a task. Thus, information about how to teach a specific skill can be determined. Specific guidelines for conducting error analyses in the area of reading, math, and spelling were included. Basically, error analysis involves the following: sampling the student's work; identifying the errors and retesting; interviewing the student; and recording the results.

From this, corrective instructional strategies can be determined
and student performance evaluated. The following topics should be
emphasized:

  *the development of CRTs (principles and procedures)

  *what to teach v. how to teach

  *error analysis in reading, spelling, and math

ACTIVITIES

5-1 DEVELOPMENT OF A CRITERION-REFERENCED TEST

Purpose - To give the student practice at task analysis, item
analysis, item construction, and determining appropriate criteria.
Description - (1) Tell students to identify a particular skill area
in mathematics, such as the addition of two-digit numbers with
carrying (e.g., 58 + 23). (2) Students are to identify objectives
by performing a task analysis on the specific skill area; assume
that the CRT will be used with a second-grade student with a
learning disability who is having particular difficulty with math.
(3) Students should develop 5-10 test items to measure each step in
the task analysis. (4) Student should indicate criteria for
acceptable responses for each step in the task analysis.

5-2 ERROR ANALYSIS IN ARITHMETIC
Purpose - To give student an opportunity to review and determine
specific error patterns and subsequently to identify appropriate
instructional objectives.
Description - Given the following problems (see Exhibit 5-2),
student should identify the type of error pattern for each example.
In addition, an instructional objective for each example should be
identified (as determined by the error analysis).

Answers -
  Example 1 - incorrect operation (child added instead of
  subtracted)
  Example 2 - computational error (child has difficulty with
  multiplication facts specifically related to the seven's table)
  Example 3 defective algorithm (child knows multiplication facts
  but applies them incorrectly)
  Example 4 - incorrect treatment of decimals (child either omits
  decimal or places the decimal in an incorrect place).

5-3 ERROR ANALYSIS IN SPELLING

Purpose - To give the student an opportunity to analyze types and other patterns of spelling errors.
Description - Given the following misspelled words (see Exhibit 5-3), students will indicate the type of error that was made.

Answers

1.substitution	6. insertion/addition	11. doubling
2.omission	7. homonym	12. omission
3.doubling	8. transposition	13. insertion/addition
4.omission	9. transposition	14. unclassified
5.substitution	10.substitution	15. substitution

5-4 DEVELOPMENT, ADMINISTRATION AND INTERPRETATION OF A CRITERION-REFERENCED TEST

Purpose - To develop, administer and interpret a criterion-referenced test.
Description - Using the steps delineated in Activity 5-1, students should develop a criterion-referenced test designed specifically for an examinee that is chosen by the student. (Note: If the CRT developed in Activity 5-1 is appropriate for the examinee, it can be used). The CRT should be administered to the examinee at a convenient time. Results of the test should then be interpreted. This should include a visual display of the results as well as short-term objectives, general objectives and general goals that are indicated. (Note: Instructor should approve the CRT and be provided evidence of parent permission prior to the test administration.)

MULTIPLE CHOICE QUESTIONS

150. A task analysis
    a) must have at least 20 steps
    *b) is generally easier for nonacademic skills than for academic skills
    c) does not have to include sequential steps
    d) is a statistical procedure

151. In addition to establishing the criteria level for mastery, a person developing a criterion-referenced test should also indicate
    a) the number of individuals in the normative sample
    *b) the number of times the student must meet the criterion level
    c) the age range for the test
    d) the ethnic status of the normative sample

152. Miscue analysis provides information in the areas of
    a) spelling and phonetic analysis
    b) addition and subtraction
    c) receptive and expressive language
   *d) oral reading and reading comprehension

153. The most common types of spelling errors are
   *a) phonetic (phonological) substitutions and omissions
    b) doubling and insertions
    c) transpositions and confused pronunciation
    d) homonyms and unclassified

154. Error analysis in mathematics is somewhat easier than the
    analysis of reading errors because
    a) more students have math problems
    b) teachers generally feel more confident 'n teaching math
   *c) a written product is available for analysis
    d) teachers can be trained to do math analysis, whereas
       reading analysis must be done by psychologists

155. Criterion-referenced tests, compared to norm-referenced
    tests
   *a) provide more specific information for developing goals
       and objectives
    b) are based on the performance of the standardization
       sample
    c) are only appropriate in academic skill areas
    d) provide scaled scores

156. Criteria for mastery in a criterion-referenced test are
    usually related to the student's
   *a) accuracy
    b) grade equivalent
    c) former experiences
    d) academic skills

157. Criterion-referenced testing is most effective when
    a) the results are used to compare students
    b) commercially prepared tests are used
   *c) it focuses on a specific set of instructional objectives
    d) it covers a broad range of areas

158. The objectives in a criterion-referenced test should include
    a) only the skill
    b) student's current level of functioning
    c) only the skill and performance level
   *d) the conditions and standards

159. Criterion-referenced testing uses a(n) _____
     approach to gather information
     a) comparative
     b) synthetic
    *c) direct
     d) indirect

160. The standards of performance in a CRT refer to
    *a) the level of performance required for mastery
     b) the mean of a standardization sample
     c) the situation under which performance is evaluated
     d) the typical results of a student

161. In evaluating the results of a properly prepared
     criterion-referenced test,
     a) inferences about the specific objective are required
     b) the evaluator must review test items
     c) the scores must be compared with others
    *d) very few inferences are necessary

162. One area that is often overlooked in criterion-referenced
     testing is
     a) the number of items on the test
     b) the specific objectives for the test
     c) the difficulty of test items
    *d) the proper instructions on how to take the test

163. The scoring of a criterion-referenced test is dependent on
    *a) the type of items used and the purpose for testing
     b) the objectives of the test and their conditions
     c) the age of the student and the allotted test time
     d) the conditions and number of objectives

164. The goal of a criterion-referenced test is
     a) to provide a general description of a student
     b) to compare how individuals perform on the test
    *c) to provide specific information for instructional
        purposes
     d) to provide general information about a student's
        performance

165. One of the limitations of CRTs is that they
     a) frequently provide little information about what to teach
    *b) frequently provide little information about how to teach
     c) are designed for a single objective
     d) are designed to measure processing

166. In order to maximize the usefulness of error analysis
    a) only one of the student's tests should be reviewed
    b) several students should be analyzed at one time
    c) only CRTs should be evaluated
   *d) a single subject area for one student should be analyzed

TRUE-FALSE QUESTIONS

167. Criterion-referenced testing requires a clearly defined domain of learning tasks. T

168. Criterion-referenced testing does not require that standards of performance be specified. F

169. The criteria used in a criterion-referenced test are always the same. F

170. A consistent coding or notation system should be used when analyzing reading errors. T

171. The mistakes made by students with learning disabilities in subtraction are generally random errors. F

172. It is usually necessary to administer all of the items in a criterion-referenced test. F

173. "Joe scored at the 43rd percentile in arithmetic" is typical of information obtained from a criterion-referenced test. F

174. "Susie can subtract one-digit numbers with 90% accuracy" is typical of information obtained from a criterion-referenced test. T

175. Error analyses in mathematics that involve the "diagnostic interview" involves gathering background information about the student. F

176. A task analysis must have at least 20 steps. F

177. A task analysis for a student with profound mental retardation would focus on a larger set of skills than one for a student with learning disabilities. F

178. In miscue analysis, the patterns of error are studied both qualitatively and quantitatively. T

37

179. The pattern of errors that a student has made can yield information pertaining to appropriate teaching strategies. T

180. In math error analysis, the computational error chart indicates only the number of errors that are made. F

181. Identifying and applying normative standards in math error analysis is similar to the comparisons that are made in norm-referenced testing. F

182. Error analysis is a procedure with which classroom teachers feel comfortable in implementing. F

183. It is best practice to use isolated spelling words as samples in spelling error analysis. F

184. In spelling error analysis, the whole word approach is the most logical for typical classroom use. T

OPEN-ENDED QUESTIONS AND DISCUSSION TOPICS

185. What is a task analysis? How is it used in developing a criterion-referenced test?

186. Describe procedures that you would use to perform a miscue analysis.

Item #	Page #	Item #	Page #
150.	92	168.	91
151.	93	169.	93
152.	101	170.	102
153.	110	171.	106
154.	103	172.	98
155.	90,91	173.	91
156.	95	174.	91
157.	91	175.	106
158.	93	176.	92
159.	94	177.	93
160.	93	178.	103
161.	94	179.	101
162.	97	180.	107
163.	98	181.	109
164.	91	182.	101
165.	100	183.	110
166.	101	184.	111
167.	91		

Exhibit 5-2

Example 1

```
   3        4        9       12       18
  +2       -1       -1       +4       -6
   5        5       10       16       24

  23       36       68       92       87
 +14      -19      -34      +84      -78
  37       55      102      176      165
```

Example 2

```
   6        4        9        8        7
  x8       x.       x5       x3       x9
  48       26       45       24       61

  19       17       14       18       16
  x6       x.8      x9       x.8      x.7
 114      140      126      144      118
```

Example 3

```
   8        9        7        9       11
  x2       x3       x.7      x.8      x9
  16       27       49       72       99

  18       16       28       39       82
  x5       x9       x.8      x.7      x.7
 540      954     1664     2163     4812
```

Example 4

```
   .2       .9       .6      .94      1.5
  +.4      -.3      +.8     +.86      -.3
   .6       .6      .14     .180      .12

$2.84      89     10.6      982    $9.14
-$1.93    +68     -8.4     -361   +$6.82
 $.91     157      .22      621   $.1596
```

39

Exhibit 5-3

For each misspelled word, indicate the type of error that was made (e.g., omission, substitution).

1.
   enuff (enough) _____

2.
   belive (believe) _____

3.
   mottel (motel) _____

4.
   nerv (nerve) _____

5.
   haz (has) _____

6.
   goode (good) _____

7.
   ate (eight) _____

8.
   towle (towel) _____

9.
   grils (girls) _____

10.
   posishun (position) _____

11.
   boddy (body) _____

12.
   thum (thumb) _____

13.
   youthe (youth) _____

14.
   vadjub (vegetable) _____

15.
   sentance (sentence) _____

Chapter 6

Curriculum-Based Assessment

Curriculum-based assessment (CBA) has been increasingly emphasized in recent years. It involves the measurement of the performance level of a student in terms of the curriculum that is being used. There are informal CBAs as well as those that are more formal and standardized. In this chapter, criterion-referenced CBA and curriculum-based measurement (CBM) were discussed.

The criterion-referenced CBA is actually a CRT with the content of the curriculum determining the content of the instrument. As such, it is based on a task-analytic model, and can be developed for any type of curriculum. The primary advantage of this informal CBA is in allowing increased instructional decision making. Other strengths of this model were discussed as well as several limitations.

Curriculum-based measurement is a standardized, empirically derived version of CBA. That is, it uses a standardized methodology with documented reliability and validity. The annual curriculum is the focus of CBM. Moreover, this procedure heavily relies on visual representations of data to determine progress and to make instructional decisions. In addition, computer-based CBMs have become popular in assisting teachers with the assessment process. Advantages and limitations of this model were also

41

discussed in this chapter. The following should be highlighted:

*development of a criterion-referenced C.B.A. instrument

*characteristics of the C.B.M. model

*visual representations of data in the C.B.M. model

*computer based C.B.M.

*an integrated model of C.B.A. and C.B.M.

*the APPLY model

*uses and limitations of both C.B.A. and C.B.M.

ACTIVITIES

7-1 DEVELOPMENT OF A CURRICULUM-BASED ASSESSMENT INSTRUMENT
Purpose - To determine how to make a C.B.A. instrument.
Description - Provide each student with several pages of a math curriculum. Instruct the students to develop a C.B.A. instrument including test items and a summary sheet using the model found in this chapter.

MULTIPLE CHOICE QUESTIONS

187. It has been suggested that curriculum-based measurement can be used
    a) as an alternative to traditional intelligence tests
    b) as an alternative to traditional achievement tests
    c) with minority students
    *d) all of the above

188. Most criterion-referenced C.B.A. procedures are based on
    a) behavioral analysis
    b) commercial programs
    *c) task-analysis
    d) standardized testing

189. C.B.M. has proven to be useful for all these areas except
    a) instructional decisions
    b) grouping for instruction
    c) identification for reintegration into the classroom
    *d) all of the above are uses of C.B.M.

190. The recommendation for administering a C.B.A. instrument is
    a) the same test three times on the same day
  *b) three separate tests on three separate days
    c) three separate tests on the same day
    d) the same test on three separate days

191. Developing criterion referenced curriculum-based assessment
    involves
    a) completing a psychological evaluation of the student
    b) prioritizing objectives
  *c) identifying skills to be measured, objectives, and
      standards of performance
    d) identifying objectives for a single student

192. Which of the following is not considered to be a strength of
    the C.B.A. model
    a) it allows increased instructional decision making
    b) it is an effective communication tool with parents
    c) it has the ability to lead to student improvement
  *d) it focuses on the product of learning

193. Curriculum-based measurement is
  *a) a standardized, empirically-derived version of C.B.A.
    b) the more informal and nonstandardized C.B.A.
    c) easily developed by the classroom teacher
    d) a commercialized criterion-referenced test

194. One of the characteristics of the C.B.M. model is
    a) a series of short-term curricular steps
    b) individualized objectives
  *c) one long-term annual goal
    d) measurement of nonstandard behaviors

195. In the C.B.M. model, instructional decisions are made based
    upon
    a) comparative score with other standardized tests
    b) the scores of the three C.B.M. tests
    c) short-term curricular objectives
  *d) the student's progress within the curriculum

196. To better determine a student's performance in C.B.M., the
    established goal is compared with
    a) other students achievement
  *b) the trend line of graphed data points
    c) the performance of students within the same curricular
      area
    d) the student's current level of functioning

197. Part of the C.B.M. procedures is
   *a) continuous assessment
    b) annual evaluation
    c) a psychological profile
    d) peer-referencing

198. Which of the following is not included in the software of
    Monitoring Basic Skills Progress?
    a) visual representation of student's scores
    b) series of short tests at a given grade level
   *c) estimation of grade equivalent
    d) feedback to the student

199. C.B.M. procedures have been supported especially for
    a) determining long-term goals
   *b) enhancing instructional decision making
    c) reading curricula
    d) math curricula

200. The C.B.M. model has been criticized for
    a) its reliability
    b) its inadequacy as an assessment method
   *c) oversimplifying the learning process
    d) lack of empirical data

201. If a student's progress is steeper than the goal line, the
    teacher
    a) discontinues assessment
   *b) increases the goal
    c) changes the instructional program
    d) moves on to a new curricular area

202. In order to determine the standards of performance for a
    criterion-referenced C.B.A., the criteria are based on
    a) scores from standardized test
    b) the student's IEP
    c) classroom achievement
   *d) the student's performance on the three tests together

203. One relatively simple method of determining a progress line
    is the _____ method.
    a) multiple baseline
   *b) quarter intersect
    c) alternate form
    d) regression

204. Curriculum-based assessment is a general term that refers to a number of models or procedures. T

205. C.B.A. involves measuring the level of a student in terms of the expected curricular outcomes of the school. T

206. The current emphasis on full inclusion of students with disabilities in the general education classroom has led to increased use of C.B.A. procedures. T

207. Greater student achievement is noted when consultation is provided for teachers when analyzing C.B.M. data. T

208. C.B.A. tests are most frequently administered individually. _ T

209. Summary sheets allow the teacher to determine the specific concepts to be tested, the number of items that measure each objective, and the standards of performance. T

210. The validity of the curriculum on which a C.B.A. instrument is based does not effect the validity of the instrument. F

211. Determining a student's progress line is more important in criterion-referenced C.B.A. than in C.B.M. F

212. The APPLY model is a combination of both criterion-referenced C.B.A. and C.B.M. T

213. Criterion referenced C.B.A. can be used with developmental curricula but not spiraling curricula. F

214. Curriculum-based measurement focuses measurement on short-term curricular steps. F

215. C.B.M. utilizes a standardized methodology with documented reliability and validity. T

216. The C.B.M. model can accommodate any instructional paradigm. T

217. If the trend line indicates that the progress is faster than the expected goal, then different instructional approaches used. F

218. The split-middle method can be used to increase the reliability of the progress line. T

219. If the student's progress is less steep than the goal line, then the teacher changes the goal. **F**

220. <u>Monitoring Basic Skills Progress</u> includes guidelines to help teachers formulate instructional decisions by interpreting graphs and skill profiles. **T**

221. Criterion-referenced C.B.A. is "a set of standard, simple short duration fluency measures". **F**

<u>OPEN-ENDED QUESTIONS OR DISCUSSION TOPICS</u>

222. What are the advantages and limitations of criterion-referenced C.B.A.? Curriculum-based measurement?

223. Compare and contrast criterion-referenced C.B.A. and C.B.M.

Item #	Page #	Item #	Page #
187.	126	205.	114
188.	115	206.	114
189.	126,127	207.	127
190.	116.	208.	116
191.	116-118	209.	117
192.	120	210.	120
193.	120	211.	121.
194.	120	212.	128
195.	120	213.	115
196.	121	214.	120
197.	123,124	215.	120
198.	125	216.	115
199.	126	217.	123
200.	127	218.	121
201.	123	219.	123
202.	118	220.	125
203.	121	221.	120
204.	115		

Chapter 7

Portfolio Assessment and Other

Alternative Procedures

In recent years, a number of assessment procedures have been used as "alternatives" to traditional norm-referenced testing. These procedures include performance assessment, authentic assessment, and portfolio assessment. Their common theme is that they all measure the student's achievement as an ongoing process and require the student to produce, demonstrate, or perform a response instead of just providing an answer. Specifically, performance assessment requires the student to perform some activity that demonstrates that he or she has mastered the competencies necessary to perform a task. The emphasis is on the practical application of learned information. Performance assessment becomes authentic assessment when it is set in a real life context.

Both performance and authentic assessment are frequently used for "high stakes" purposes, such as school district wide evaluation. Proponents argue that these types of assessment are better suited to measure students' learning. Critics point out that these tests frequently lack acceptable technical characteristics and are costly and time consuming to prepare.

Perhaps the most directly applicable alternative assessment procedure for the teacher is portfolio assessment. This involves a collection of the student's work that provides examples of his or her efforts in a particular area. The portfolio can be assembled to show the student's best work, typical work, etc. In other words, a portfolio can be assembled for different purposes. The following points should be emphasized in this chapter:

   *the reasons why alternative assessment has become popular

   *the similarities and differences between performance and authentic assessment

   *the distinction between high stakes and low stakes assessment

   *the advantages and limitations of performance and authentic assessment

   *purposes for portfolio assessment

   *steps in developing a portfolio

   *developing a rubric

ACTIVITIES

7-1 DEVELOPING A PERFORMANCE ASSESSMENT
Purpose - To provide the student with an opportunity to construct a performance-based assessment test.
Description - Have the students, working in small groups, develop a performance task that would measure the concept of multiplication of two digit numbers. Have them refer to the Fuchs (1994) example from the chapter to provide some ideas. Each group should share their performance task with the rest of the class.

7-2 DEVELOPING A PORTFOLIO
Purpose - To learn how to construct a portfolio.
Description - As a take home assignment, have the students review the steps in developing a portfolio (the example in the chapter outlines each step). They should then provide their own example of the development of a portfolio for a fourth grade student in the area of reading. Special attention should be given to the purpose for the portfolio and making sure that the entries match

with the purpose.

<u>MULTIPLE CHOICE QUESTIONS</u>

224. There has been growing dissatisfaction with norm-referenced achievement tests. Which of the following is <u>not</u> a criticism?
    a) too much value placed on recall
    *b) difficult to administer to groups
    c) promotes the impression that there is only one correct response
    d) turns students into passive learners

225. Alternative assessment approaches include all except
    a) performance assessment
    b) authentic assessment
    *c) kinetic assessment
    d) portfolio assessment

226. Reasons for using performance assessment include
    a) determination and evaluation of objectives
    b) gathering of prereferral information
    c) monitoring progress
    *d) all of the above

227. High stakes assessment includes
    a) determination of objectives
    b) determination of goals
    *c) determination of student promotion
    d) determination of teaching strategies

228. Performance assessment has been criticized because
    a) it is expensive
    b) it is difficult to keep the answers secure
    c) it frequently lacks validity and reliability data
    *d) all of the above

229. Which of the following is true?
    a) performance and authentic assessment are always the same
    b) performance and authentic assessment are never the same
    *c) some performance assessment can be authentic
    d) some authentic assessment is performance-based

230. Which of the following is not a characteristic of portfolio assessment?
    *a) sample collected during a single testing session
    b) data generated from multiple procedures
    c) samples come from natural contexts
    d) includes actual work and summary information

231. The _____ Education Reform Act includes a statewide portfolio project.
    a) Michigan
    b) Massachusetts
    c) Virginia
    *d) Kentucky

232. The working portfolio is also referred to as the
    a) show portfolio
    *b) instructional portfolio
    c) educational portfolio
    d) evaluation portfolio

233. Portfolio assessment has been used to identify minority students as
    a) having a learning disability
    b) having English as a second language
    *c) gifted
    d) being ready to enter kindergarten

234. Included in any portfolio should be
    a) at least ten entries
    b) results of a standardized test
    c) written work product
    *d) student self reflection

235. A _____ is frequently developed to help evaluate portfolio material.
    a) yardstick
    b) criterion-referenced test
    *c) rubric
    d) rating scale

236. Using examples of work to illustrate the various levels of accomplishment in a portfolio is called
    a) objectifying
    *b) benchmarking
    c) mastering
    d) demonstrating

237. Which of the following is important in determining the contents of a portfolio?
    a) purpose
    b) audience
    c) type of entries
    *d) all of the above

238. Which is not an important question to ask before developing a portfolio?
    a) What should it look like?
    b) What goes in?
    *c) How do I purge the information?
    d) How do I pass the portfolio on?

239. The primary use of portfolio assessment is for
    *a) low stakes purposes
    b) high stakes purposes
    c) determining grades
    d) choosing a curriculum

240. Which of the following is not a change that has been taking place in the assessment field?
    a) assessment becoming holistic and dynamic
    *b) assessment becoming specific and static
    c) assessment becoming multidimensional
    d) assessment becoming more continuous

TRUE-FALSE QUESTIONS

241. Performance assessment is a newly developed form of assessment. F

242. One of the difficulties of using performance assessment for large scale purposes is keeping the content of the exams secure. T

243. Performance assessment becomes authentic assessment when it is set in a real life context. T

244. The distinction between performance and authentic assessment is relatively clear in the classroom. F

245. Of all the alternative assessment procedures, portfolio assessment has the most direct relevance for the classroom teacher. T

246. Portfolio assessment is a skill by skill approach that focuses primarily on the product of learning. F

51

247. A portfolio should contain a table of contents that organizes the materials into sections. T

248. A portfolio should begin and end with each new school year and teacher. F

249. The actual content of the portfolio will depend on its purpose. T

250. Because of the subjective nature of alternative assessment approaches, reliability is not a concern. F

251. High stakes assessment results in the development of an individualized education program. F

252. A benchmark is used to increase the reliability of a rubric. T

253. Writing a letter to the editor of a local newsletter is an example of authentic assessment of written expression. T

254. One disadvantage of portfolio assessment is that it cannot be integrated with classroom instruction. F

255. A working portfolio and a show portfolio are used for the same purpose. F

256. The Grady Profile is an expandable file folder that can be used to organize students' worksheets. F

257. It is possible to combine portfolio assessment with C.B.M. to develop and evaluate instructional programs. T

258. In general, the more criteria used in a rubric, the easier it is to use. F

OPEN-ENDED QUESTIONS OR DISCUSSION TOPICS

259. What are the similarities and differences between performance assessment and authentic assessment?

260. What steps should be followed to develop a show portfolio for a third grade student with learning disabilities in the area of multiplication?

Chapter 8

Assessment of Intelligence

OVERVIEW AND TEACHING SUGGESTIONS

The area of intelligence testing is controversial. There are
those who strongly support the use of intelligence tests and base
many educational decisions on their results. On the other hand,
there are those who would prefer to ban the use of all
intelligence tests in school. Perhaps a more moderate/pragmatic
position is in order. Many intelligence tests do predict how
well a student will perform in school. They do not, however,
measure some innate intellectual potential. (Several alternative
approaches designed to measure "potential" were also discussed.)
We must be aware of the limitations of intelligence tests and not
"overinterpret" the results. In special education they can be
helpful in making eligibility and placement decisions as well as
in identifying general strengths and weaknesses. The following
points should be emphasized in this chapter:

*problems in defining intelligence

*difficulties in measuring intelligence

*the incorrect use of intelligence tests to measure
  "learning potential"

*the use and limitation of IQs in eligibility decisions

*global vs. single skill characteristics of various
  instruments

<u>ACTIVITY</u>

8-1 CLASS DISCUSSION OF INTELLIGENCE
<u>Purpose</u> - To demonstrate to students the difficulty in defining
intelligence which in turn influences the measurement of
intelligence.
<u>Description</u> - Allow students in small groups 10 minutes to
develop their own definition of intelligence. Next, request
students to read their definition to the class. At the same
time, the instructor should outline the various responses on the
blackboard. Topics for discussion should include the
similarities and differences, "global" vs. "single skill"
definitions and how the definitions correspond with currently
used instruments.

<u>MULTIPLE CHOICE QUESTIONS</u>

261. Group intelligence tests should primarily be used
     a) for placement decisions
    *b) for rough screening purposes
     c) for the diagnosis of mental retardation
     d) to determine specific instructional strategies

262. The Detroit Tests of Learning Aptitude-4
    *a) provides scores for three major domains
     b) is a group intelligence test
     c) is an adult aptitude test for mechanical reasoning and
        numerical ability
     d) is a "culturally fair" test

263. The WISC-III provides
     a) a Mental Age score and a ratio IQ
     b) percentile scores for reading and mathematics
    *c) Verbal, Performance, and Full Scale IQS
     d) Verbal and Quantitative IQS

264. Which of the following domains is <u>not</u> found on the Detroit
     Test of Learning Aptitude-4?
     a) linguistic
    *b) performance
     c) attentional
     d) motoric

265. The Optimal Mental Ability Score from the DTLA-4 is computed
     from
     a) scores from all the subtests
    *b) the four highest subtest scores
     c) scores from three subtests of the examiner's choosing
     d) the highest domain score

266. The Learning Potential Assessment Strategy is
    a) a group intelligence test
    b) a static assessment device
    *c) a test-train-retest system of assessment
    d) a system developed to assess the gifted

267. Arguments to move away from traditional intelligence tests
    include all of the following except
    a) they are more concerned with products rather than the
       processes of learning
    *b) group administration is difficult
    c) they do not address the individual's response to
       instruction
    d) they do not provide prescriptive information

268. The WISC-III
    a) can be used with preschool children
    b) can be used with adults
    *c) can be used with school age students
    d) all of the above

269. The Learning Potential Assessment Strategy, Learning
    Potential Assessment Device, and Paired-Associate
    Learning techniques
    a) are all static assessment techniques
    *b) are all dynamic assessment techniques
    c) have been used exclusively with students with learning
       disabilities
    d) have been thoroughly discredited in the special education
       community

270. The WISC-III provides an Index score for the area of
    a) verbal expression
    *b) freedom from distractibility
    c) receptive language
    d) long-term memory

271. Which of the following statements is true regarding the
    Stanford Binet Intelligence Scale-4?
    a) Its global score should not be used
    b) It does not include memory tasks
    *c) It is based on a three level hierarchical model
    d) It yields a verbal and performance IQ

272. Dynamic assessment is <u>not</u> characterized by which of the following?
    a) test-teach-test paradigm
    *b) emphasis on assessment of product not process
    c) attempts to specify obstacles to more effective learning
    d) attempts to distinguish between performance and potential

273. The use of paired-associate learning is based on the assumption that
    a) meaningful association facilitates learning
    b) the ability to make meaningful associations indicates intelligence
    *c) learning new material is a good indication of learning ability
    d) reading is a good indication of intelligence

274. Which test should be used more for screening purposes?
    *a) Slosson Intelligence Test-Revised
    b) Detroit Tests of Learning Aptitude-4
    c) Wechsler Intelligence Scale for Children-III
    d) Stanford Binet Intelligence Scale-4

275. The WISC-III has a linking standardization sample with a(n) _____ test also authored by Wechsler.
    *a) achievement
    b) adaptive behavior
    c) language
    d) perceptual-motor

276. Research on the Stanford-Binet-4 indicates that gifted students score _____ on the SB-4 as compared to the Wechsler Intelligence Scale for Children-Revised.
    a) about the same
    b) generally higher
    *c) considerably lower
    d) slightly better

277. Which of the following tests measures a number of components of intelligence?
    a) Goodenough-Harris Drawing Test
    b) Kaufman Brief Intelligence Test
    *c) McCarthy Scales of Children's Abilities
    d) Slosson Intelligence Test-Revised

TRUE-FALSE QUESTIONS

278. The exact meaning of the four Index scores from the WISC-III is unclear. <u>T</u>

279. Traditional intelligence tests measure intellectual potential. F

280. The Stanford-Binet-4 has acceptable validity and reliability. T

281. In general, scores from verbally oriented intelligence tests are relatively good predictors of achievement test scores. T

282. Traditional intelligence tests are referred to as static assessments. T

283. The Stanford-Binet-4 fits into a hierarchical model that includes fluid and crystallized intelligence. T

284. The global composite score is the most reliable measure of learning aptitude on the Detroit Tests of Learning Aptitude-4. T

285. It is appropriate to compare composite scores from different domains from the DTLA-4. F

286. Group-administered intelligence tests are very similar in structure and format to group-administered achievement tests. T

287. Many researchers, including Gardner, feel that intelligence is defined primarily as verbal ability. F

288. The WISC-III has 10 subtests and 3 optional subtests. T

289. The WISC-III yields higher scores than the WISC-R. F

290. One of the cited purposes for constructing the Stanford Binet-4 was to help identify students with behavior disorders. F

291. The WISC-III, like all of Weschler's scales, is based on the concept of global intelligence. T

292. Intelligence tests have been developed specifically for individuals with physical or sensory deficits. T

293. The Slosson Full Range Intelligence Test measures similar areas as the Stanford-Binet-4. T

294. Although the Kaufman Brief Intelligence Test has adequate technical characteristics, it only includes a measure of verbal intelligence. F

295. The Stanford-Binet-4 yields similar scores as other intelligence tests with gifted children. **F**

OPEN-ENDED QUESTIONS OR DISCUSSION TOPICS

296. What factors should be considered in the selection of an intelligence test for a six year old child? Your response should encompass technical characteristics as well as factors related to the referral and the age of the child.

297. Briefly discuss the "nature-nurture" controversy related to intelligence testing. Why is this issue vigorously debated?

Item #	Page #	Item #	Page #
261.	161	279.	158
262.	163	280.	170
263.	172	281.	158
264.	163	282.	158
265.	163	283.	165
266.	159	284.	165
267.	159	285.	165
268.	170	286.	161
269.	159,160	287.	158
270.	172	288.	170
271.	165	289.	177
272.	159	290.	165
273.	160	291.	170
274.	179	292.	161
275.	177	293.	179
276.	168	294.	178
277.	179	295.	169
278.	177		

Chapter 9

Assessment of Adaptive Behavior

OVERVIEW AND TEACHING SUGGESTIONS

Adaptive behavior scales are used for a variety of purposes.
They may used to assist in the eligibility process, to help develop
educational objectives for students with moderate to severe
disabilities, and/or to evaluate specific teaching programs.
Adaptive behavior instruments traditionally have been used with
individuals with mental retardation or those suspected of having
mental retardation although many of the tests have relevance for
other types of students. Most adaptive behavior measures include
items in the area of independent functioning, self-help skills,
sensory and motor skills, communication skills, and social skills.
For the most part the nature and subsequent measurement of adaptive
behavior is related. For example, adaptive behavior would be
defined differently for a three year old child than for a thirteen
year old student. From a technical point of view the reliability
and validity of many of these tests have been questioned. Perhaps
this is partially due to their format that often requires an
interview or limited observation. The following issues are of
particular importance in this chapter:

   *the importance of adaptive behavior in the classification of
      mental retardation

*general problems of lack of validity and reliability of many

  of the instruments

*the various data collection procedures used (interview,

  observational) and the advantages and disadvantages of each

*various uses of adaptive behavior scales (depending in part

  on the characteristics of the normative population).

*use of adaptive behavior scales for descriptive

  (eligibility) vs. prescriptive (educational programming)

  purposes

*importance of the nature of the informant (e.g., teacher vs.

  parent) on the results obtained

ACTIVITIES

9-1 MEASUREMENT OF ADAPTIVE BEHAVIOR USING THE SIB-R

Purpose - To provide the student with the opportunity to administer
the SIB-R to facilitate the development of effective interview
skills and to determine differences in scores based on the nature
of the informant.
Description - Given a SIB-R manual, students will be required to
observe a child and administer the SIB-R to the child's parent(s)
and teacher. Upon completion, students will complete a report
including results and an interpretation of the findings, focusing
on the similarities and differences of the responses from the
different sources.

9-2 CHOOSING AGE-APPROPRIATE ADAPTIVE BEHAVIOR INSTRUMENTS

Purpose - To help students learn to choose appropriate adaptive
behavior instruments.
Description - As a take-home assignment, give students a list of
specific adaptive behavior instruments along with the
characteristics and home environments of four special education
students (see Exhibit 10-2). Have students decide which of the
listed instruments would be the most appropriate to administer for
each student. They should defend their decisions.

61

Possible Answers: Joan - Vineland or ABS-S2
                    Harry - Vineland or ABS-RC2
                    Susan - NABC
                    Tom - AAA

MULTIPLE CHOICE QUESTIONS

298. The Assessment of Adaptive Areas was developed specifically
     to address
     a) the IQ of an individual
     b) the specific instructional concerns of students
    *c) the adaptive behavior components in the AAMR definition
     d) the declassification of minority students

299. Which one of the following statements is true regarding the
     AAMR Adaptive Behavior Scale-2?
     a) teachers don't rate children's adaptive behavior
    *b) parents tend to rate their children's adaptive behavior
        differently than teachers
     c) parents and teachers rate children's adaptive behavior
        equally
     d) parents and teacher never rate the same child's adaptive
        behavior

300. Adaptive behavior
     a) refers to intellectual potential
    *b) is included in the AAMR definition for mental retardation
     c) is best measured by intelligence tests
     d) is primarily an important consideration during the
        preschool years

301. Part Two of the AAMR Adaptive Behavior Scales-2 focuses on
     a) self help skills
     b) estimated learning potential (ELP)
    *c) maladaptive behavior
     d) pre-vocational skills

302. Which instrument includes a separate component for classroom
     teacher observation of adaptive behavior?
     a) Scales of Independent Behavior-Revised
     b) Assessment of Adaptive Areas
    *c) Vineland Adaptive Behavior Scales
     d) Adaptive Behavior Scale-School Edition

303. The purpose for which an adaptive behavior test can be used depends largely on
    a) the teacher's expertise as an examiner
    *b) the characteristics of the instrument's standardization sample
    c) the cooperation of the children being assessed
    d) the gender of the examines

304. Which of the following statements about the Kaufman Functional Academic Skills Test is not true
    a) the individual must actually perform each skill
    b) it measures functional reading and math skills
    *c) it can be used with preschool children
    d) it was conormed with the Kaufman Brief Intelligence Test

305. The Vineland Adaptive Behavior Scales include
    *a) three separate editions that can be combined or used separately
    b) a series of true-false questions
    c) a screening edition
    d) a section that the child completes

306. The Normative Adaptive Behavior Checklist
    *a) provides a quick estimate of adaptive behavior
    b) is an in-depth system of assessing independent living skills
    c) is a screening device which can indicate that a child needs a more thorough testing with the Vineland Adaptive Behavior Scales
    d) has limited reliability and validity

307. Which of the following types of skills is not found on the Responsibility and Independence Scale for Adolescents?
    a) money management
    *b) toileting skills
    c) transportation
    d) career development

308. Which of the following is an advantage of the Adaptive Behavior Inventory?
    a) it is quickly and easily administered by parents
    b) it has strong evidence of validity
    *c) it includes persons with and without disabilities in the norming sample
    d) all of the above

309. The instrument for assessing adaptive behavior that has an associated curriculum and criterion-referenced checklist is the
    a) Kaufman Functional Academic Skills Test
    *b) Scales of Independent Behavior-Revised
    c) Vineland Adaptive Behavior Scales
    d) none of the above

310. In order to score the Assessment of Adaptive Areas it is first necessary to administer which adaptive behavior scale?
    a) Adaptive Behavior Inventory
    *b) AAMR Adaptive Behavior Scale-2
    c) Adaptive Behavior Inventory for Children
    d) Vineland Adaptive Behavior Scales

311. Part one of the AAMR Adaptive Behavior Scales assesses
    a) maladaptive behavior
    *b) independence in daily living skills
    c) both a& b
    d) none of the above

312. Which of the following adaptive behavior instruments should be used for screening purposes only?
    *a) Kaufman Functional Academic Skills Test
    b) Vineland Adaptive Behavior Scale
    c) both a & b
    d) neither a nor b

313. Which of the following is a general purpose for which adaptive behavior evaluation instruments can be used?
    a) making eligibility decisions
    b) developing and evaluating specific teaching programs
    c) screening
    *d) all of the above

314. One criticism of adaptive behavior instruments is that they generally lack validity, particularly
    a) concurrent validity
    b) content validity
    *c) predictive validity
    d) all of the above

315. Which of the following instruments provide a visual representation of data obtained?
    a) Assessment of Adaptive Areas
    b) AAMR Adaptive Behavior Scale-2
    c) Neither a or b
    *d) Both a and b

316. Which of the following should <u>not</u> be used for eligibility purposes?
   a) Vineland Adaptive Behavior Scales
   b) Adaptive Behavior Inventory
  *c) Normative Adaptive Behavior Checklist
   d) Scales of Independent Behavior-Revised

TRUE-FALSE QUESTIONS

317. The AAMR ABS-S2 is used primarily for very rough screening purposes. <u>F</u>

318. Adaptive behavior has to do with a person's ability to deal effectively with personal and social demands. <u>T</u>

319. The Assessment of Adaptive Areas is a recategorization of the items from the Vineland Adaptive Behavior Scale Interview Editions. <u>F</u>

320. There is a curriculum available that is correlated with items from the Scales of Independent Behavior-Revised. <u>T</u>

321. The classroom edition of the Vineland Adaptive Behavior Scales is recommended over the interview editions.

322. The Normative Adaptive Behavior Checklist was designed as a screening version of the Comprehensive Test of Adaptive Behavior. <u>T</u>

323. Adaptive behavior tests used to help make eligibility decisions are usually standardized on a population without mental retardation. <u>T</u>

324. The Adaptive Behavior Inventory provides specific information for educational programming. <u>F</u>

325. The School Edition of the AAMR-ABS-2 is simply a longer version of the Residential and Community Edition. <u>F</u>

326. A deficit in adaptive behavior and cognitive functioning must be documented before an individual is labeled as having mental retardation. <u>T</u>

327. Specific educational plans can be developed for a student with severe mental retardation using the AAMR-ABS-S2. <u>F</u>

328. The Vineland Adaptive Behavior Scales can be used with a wide variety of individuals ranging from preschool to secondary age. <u>T</u>

329. The Adaptive Behavior Inventory for Children focuses on nonschool behavior. T

330. The Adaptive Behavior Inventory has a shorter screening version. T

OPEN-ENDED QUESTIONS OR DISCUSSION TOPICS

331. Discuss why adaptive behavior is a significant consideration with respect to eligibility decisions and educational programming.

332. What are the advantages and disadvantages of parent interviews relative to the measurement of adaptive behavior?

333. Compare and contrast the three editions of the Vineland Adaptive Behavior Scales (Expanded, Survey, & Classroom).

Item #	Page #	Item #	Page #
298.	191	315.	187,192
299.	189	316.	203
300.	182	317.	185
301.	187	318.	182
302.	198	319.	191
303.	182	320.	195
304.	203	321.	202
305.	198	322.	203
306.	203	323.	182
307.	204	324.	183
308.	185	325.	185
309.	195	326.	185
310.	194	327.	191
311.	185	328.	198
312.	203	329.	203
313.	182,183	330.	183
314.	183		

Exhibit 9-2

ADAPTIVE BEHAVIOR INSTRUMENTS

Vineland Adaptive Behavior Scales
Normative Adaptive Behavior Checklist
Assessment of Adaptive Areas
AAMR Adaptive Behavior Scale-S:2
AAMR Adaptive Behavior Scale-RC:2

STUDENTS

Joan
Joan is a three year old child who has a measured IQ of 55 on the
WPPSI-R. She lives at home with her parents and two older
siblings. She is being evaluated for admittance to a public
school early intervention program.

Harry
Harry is an eight year old child who is currently enrolled in a
general second grade classroom at a private school. His recent
evaluation by a private psychologist revealed a borderline IQ
score of 72 on the WISC-III. He lives at home with his mother
and grandmother and has no siblings. His mother is interested in
seeing if a public school program would meet his academic and
social needs.

Susan
Susan is a 22 year old young woman who resides in a residential
group home for individuals with mental retardation. She is being
evaluated to determine appropriate transitional objectives to
prepare her for employment in the community. Her counselor wants
to give her a quick screening to determine appropriate areas to
evaluate in more depth later. She has been found to have an IQ
of 45 on the WAIS-R.

Tom
Tom is a six year old Hispanic child who is enrolled in a first
grade classroom in a public school. He lives at home with both
parents and four siblings in a lower socioeconomic area. His
teacher has noted that he has been struggling in all his academic
areas. She also reports he has particular difficulty in
communication and self-help skills. His cumulative record showed
a history of failure. He was referred for special education
services and was administered the WISC-III on which he obtained
an IQ of 65.

Chapter 10

Assessment of Behavioral and Emotional Status

OVERVIEW AND TEACHING SUGGESTIONS

This chapter focuses both on techniques concerned with the
measurement of an individual's emotional state and on rating
scales that are concerned with documentation of observable
behavior. In general, the measurement of emotional status is a
highly subjective area that has extreme limitations. Several
types of procedures were discussed including: projective
techniques, measures of self concept, and inventories
/questionnaires. Individual instruments were described in each
of the three categories, and issues regarding lack of validity,
reliability and educational significance were discussed.
Behavior rating scales, although focusing on observable behavior
are also somewhat subjective; many also have limited educational
relevance. Included in this chapter were general rating scales
for the classroom/home environment, rating scales for social
skills, rating scales for ADHD, and autism rating scales. The
following topics should be highlighted in this chapter:

*limitations of many behavior rating scales (e.g. technical

  characteristics, educational relevance)

*strengths and limitations of classroom/home scales

*strengths and limitations of social skills rating scales

*strengths and limitations of ADHD scales

*strengths and limitations of autism rating scales

68

*difficulties in attempting to measure an individual's

"emotional state"

*general criticisms of projective testing

*limitations of self-concept scales and inventories/

questionnaires

ACTIVITIES

10-1 EFFECTS OF FEEDBACK ON PROJECTIVE TEST RESULTS

Purpose - To give the students insight into the effects of
reinforcement on examinee responses.
Description - Divide the class into four groups -- two examiner
groups and two examinee groups. Instruct one examiner group to
administer the word association test (see Exhibit 11-1), write
down the responses, and give no feedback to the examinee. The
other examiner group is instructed to do the same except to
verbally approve ("OK", "good", "uh-huh") any response that
includes more than one syllable. Each examiner then individually
administers the test following the prescribed instruction. After
everyone has been tested, have the examiners count the number of
polysyllabic responses and compare the results of the two groups.
A discussion should follow on the role of feedback in testing.
The discussion can be initiated by asking the examinees who were
reinforced if they realized what was happening.

10-2 ASSESSING BEHAVIOR IN THE PUBLIC SCHOOL SYSTEM (FOR
     UNDERGRADUATE STUDENTS)

Purpose - To acquaint students with behavior rating instruments
in current use in local public school systems.
Description - Have students interview a school psychologist, a
teacher of students with emotional/behavioral problems, or a
principal from the local school system (or nearby systems) to
find out what assessment instruments are currently being used to
determine eligibility or programming for students suspected of
having emotional or behavioral problems. The students should
also ask the person they interview to delineate the strengths and
weaknesses of the instrument(s), and any recommendations they
might have concerning other tests or procedure that would help
identify students with emotional and behavior problems. Students
should report their findings at a subsequent class meeting when
the tests named can be discussed.

334. The Walker Problem Behavior Identification Checklist
    a) has been widely researched
  *b) is quick to administer and score
    c) can be used to make labeling and classification decisions
    d) can be group administered

335. Which of the following is true of the Child Behavior
    Checklist (Achenbach & Edelbrock)?
    a) it is completed only by the classroom teacher
    b) it concerns only externalizing behaviors
  *c) there are separate profiles for boys and girls
    d) all of the above

336. The Devereux Behavior Rating Scale-School Form
  *a) is based on the definition of serious emotional
      disturbance used in IDEA
    b) measures only behaviors on the playground
    c) uses a pass/fail system of rating each behavior
    d) has a self-rating scale

337. Projective measures evolved from
    a) behavioral psychology
    b) experimental psychology and statistics
    c) developmental psychology and learning theory
  *d) psychoanalytic theory and gestalt psychology

338. Behavior rating scales
    a) should be administered by trained psychologists only
  *b) are typically administered by teachers
    c) require students to complete a questionnaire about
      themselves
    d) are never completed by parents

339. Which of the following behavior rating scales include
    ratings by teachers, parents, and the student?
  *a) Behavior Rating Profile-2
    b) Revised Behavior Problem Checklist
    c) Walker Problem Behavior Identification Checklist
    d) Devereux Behavior Rating Scale-School Form

340. Which of the following does not apply to the Personality
    Inventory for Children?
    a) a screening version is included
    b) it is a downward extension of the MMPI
  *c) it is most useful for designing educational programming
    d) its use with preschoolers has been criticized

341. Which of the following statements is true regarding behavior rating scales?
    a) Parents and teachers tend to rate the same child similarly
    *b) Parents and teachers tend to rate the same child differently
    c) Parents and teachers never rate the same child
    d) Parents and teachers rate the same child together

342. Personality and self-concept inventories typically use a(n) _____ format
    a) observational
    *b) self-report
    c) interview
    d) criterion-referenced

343. The MMPI-R and the Sixteen-Personality Factor are examples of
    a) projective tests
    b) self-concept scales
    *c) inventories and questionnaires
    d) behavior rating scales

344. In general, many behavior rating scales have been criticized for
    a) using the teacher as the rater
    *b) their lack of educational relevance
    c) documenting observable behavior
    d) using parents as raters

345. Which of the following does not include separate rating forms for teachers and parents?
    a) Behavior Rating Profile-2
    b) Child Behavior Checklist
    *c) Devereux Behavior Rating Scale-School Form
    d) All of the above do

346. The technical aspects of the Walker-McConnell Scale have been rated as satisfactory with the following exception:
    *a) poorly described standardization
    b) poor integrate reliability
    c) poor construct validity
    d) none of the above

347. Which of the following statements is <u>not</u> true about the
     Conners Rating Scales-Revised?
     a) There is a short form and a long form
     b) It is used to identify children with ADHD
     c) It has a teacher and parent version
     *d) It is used exclusively in the home

348. The items on the Gilliam Autism Rating Scale
     a) include the areas of communication and stereotyped
        behavior
     b) were based in part on the DSM-IV
     c) can be administered in 5-10 minutes
     *d) all of the above

TRUE-FALSE QUESTIONS

349. Inventories and questionnaires to measure emotional status
     are typically designed for use with young children. <u>F</u>

350. In general, projective techniques lack reliability and
     validity. <u>T</u>

351. The Revised Behavior Problem Checklist has a limited
     standardization sample. <u>T</u>

352. The Devereux Behavior Rating Scale uses one form for all
     ages. <u>F</u>

353. The School Social Behavior Scales include ratings of both
     social skills and problem behaviors. <u>T</u>

354. The ACTeRS is recommended to be administered to the parents
     because the items are exhibited in the home. <u>F</u>

355. The Walker Problem Behavior Identification Checklist should
     be considered a quick screening instrument. <u>T</u>

356. The Autism Screening Instrument for Educational Planning is
     a quickly administered instrument. <u>F</u>

357. Many of the categories on behavior rating scales measure
     similar behavior dimensions. <u>T</u>

358. One advantage of the Behavior and Emotional Rating Scale is
     that it focuses on the strengths rather than the weaknesses
     of the child. <u>T</u>

359. The Behavior Rating Profile-2 can help determine if a child's behavior at school is maladaptive, but it does not assess home behaviors. F

360. The Behavior Evaluation Scale-2 is more a screening instrument than a comprehensive rating scale. T

361. The Children's Attention and Adjustment Survey is a comprehensive measure of ADHD. F

362. The Emotional or Behavior Disorders Scale was designed to be consistent with the PL 94-142 definition of serious emotional disturbance. F

363. A longer, more clinical version of the Devereux Behavior rating Scale is available. T

364. The brevity of administration is one positive aspect of the Walker-McConnell Scale. T

365. The Childhood Autism Rating Scales is part of a project called TEACCH. T

366. Most instruments that measure ADHD require direct observation and data collection. F

OPEN-ENDED QUESTIONS OR DISCUSSION TOPICS

367. Compare and contrast the Revised Behavior Problem Checklist, the Behavior Rating Profile-2 and the Child Behavior Checklist

368. What is meant by "reverse projection"?

Item #	Page #	Item #	Page #
334.	222	351.	210
335.	216	352.	217
336.	217	353.	221
337.	230	354.	227
338.	207	355.	222
339.	210,211	356.	229
340.	238,239	357.	208
341.	208	358.	219
342.	235,238	359.	212
343.	239	360.	220
344.	208	361.	228
345.	216,217	362.	221

346.	225	363.	217
347.	228	364.	226
348.	230	365.	229
349.	238	366.	207
350.	231		

Exhibit 10-1

shoe	_____	old	_____	owe	_____	zoo	_____
book	_____	pie	_____	paper	_____	eat	_____
hair	_____	war	_____	gun	_____	die	_____
very	_____	able	_____	worry	_____	rock	_____
shirt	_____	cold	_____	fish	_____	fast	_____
attack	_____	help	_____	mother	_____	bed	_____
sick	_____	about	_____	until	_____	bird	_____
pain	_____	that	_____	climb	_____	team	_____
under	_____	teach	_____	current	_____	street	_____
boy	_____	rose	_____	jungle	_____	tell	_____
window	_____	time	_____	loyal	_____	size	_____
maybe	_____	short	_____	milk	_____	nice	_____
rise	_____	dress	_____	need	_____	model	_____
clock	_____	awful	_____	steam	_____	lie	_____
big	_____	seven	_____	cold	_____	kit	_____

Chapter 11

Assessment of Oral Language

OVERVIEW AND TEACHING SUGGESTIONS

Assessment of language ability is an important issue in the area of special education. Most tests are designed to measure the specific components of language - phonology, syntax (and morphology), and semantics in both the receptive and expressive channels. There are tests that also measure the area of pragmatics, or the use of language for communicative intent. One of the more widely used language tests is the Peabody Picture Vocabulary Test-III that measures the semantic-receptive component. Several tests, however, attempt to measure a combination of these language components. There are also a number or tests with which special educators should be familiar that are typically given by speech/language clinicians. The following information should be highlighted in this chapter:

   *definitions of the various components of language

   *the importance of understanding test results from tests
    administered by speech/language clinicians

   *the usefulness of assessing pragmatic aspects of language

   *strengths and limitations of single component and
    multicomponent tests

ACTIVITIES

12-1 COLLECTION AND ANALYSIS OF A LANGUAGE SAMPLE

Purpose - To provide the students with an opportunity to analyze language samples in a natural context.
Description - Have students work in small groups. Each group should obtain about a ten-minute elicited imitative language sample of a child. The students should first design the questions or stimuli used to elicit the sample. The sample should be tape recorded and transcribed. Students should be encouraged to read the two Smiley (1991) articles cited in the chapter to provide guidelines on how to analyze the sample.

12-2 ADMINISTRATION AND SCORING OF THE PEABODY PICTURE
        VOCABULARY TEST-III

Purpose - To acquaint students with a widely-used test of receptive language.
Description - Divide the class up into small groups. Supply each group with a copy of the PPVT-III. Have students take turns administering the test to each other. While one student functions as the examiner, the others may practice scoring the examinee's responses. After 20-30 minutes, have the class discuss their feelings about the test and any problems they may have encountered with the administration or scoring of it. Lead a class discussion about the strengths and limitations of the PPVT-III. Note: Students should thoroughly understand the concept of basal and ceiling rules (see Exhibit 12-2 for this exercise).

MULTIPLE CHOICE QUESTIONS

369. The Peabody Picture Vocabulary Test-III is a measure of
    a) expressive vocabulary (semantics)
    b) sentence structure (syntax)
   *c) receptive vocabulary (semantics)
    d) morphology

370. The stimulus items for the Peabody Picture Vocabulary Test-III.
    a) require a verbal response
    b) are colored photographs
   *c) allow for a pointing response
    d) are written words that the student must identify

371. Semantics refers to
    a) how morphemes are put together
    b) aural discrimination of speech sounds
    c) receptive vocabulary only
    *d) the meaning of words

372. Pragmatics refers to
    a) the functional use of language
    b) word meanings
    c) written vocabulary
    d) how sentences are put together

373. The Test of Language Competence covers the areas of
    a) syntax only
    b) semantics only
    c) pragmatics only
    *d) all of the above

374. The Clinical Evaluation of Language Fundamentals-3
    a) evaluates language processing only
    *b) evaluates language processing and production
    c) uses a written language sample along with the oral
       language subtests
    d) was normed on language-disordered preschoolers

375. Morphology refers to
    a) the smallest significant units of sound combined into
       words
    b) the relational meanings of language
    *c) how phonemes are put together to give meaning
    d) the meaning of words

376. Which of the following is not true for the Test of
     Adolescent and Adult Language-3?
    a) it is one of the few tests available for testing older
       students' language skills
    b) it includes measures of syntax and semantics
    c) it includes subtests that require writing
    *d) its validity has been well established

377. The Tests of Language Development-3 consist of
    a) an A and B edition
    b) a criterion-referenced and norm-referenced edition
    *c) a primary and an intermediate edition
    d) a preschool and elementary school edition

378. One positive feature of the Comprehensive Receptive and
     Expressive Language Test is
     a) a Spanish version is available
   * b) you can compare receptive and expressive skills with the
        same normative sample
     c) it can be used with nonverbal children
     d) it is designed for parent use

379. The Oral Scales from the OWLS
     a) measure only listening comprehension
     b) measure only oral expression
    *c) measure both listening comprehension and oral expression
     d) measure neither listening comprehension nor oral
        expression

380. The purpose of the Language Processing Test-Revised is to
     a) assess a child's vocabulary development
   * b) measure the ability to attach meaning to language and
        formulate a response
     c) quickly screen for language processing
     d) measure an individual's ability to relate to a speaker
        and understand what is being said

381. Which of the following is not a structural component of
     language?
     a) syntax
     b) phonology
     c) semantics
    *d) articulation

382. Which statement is not true about the OWLS?
     a) Additional reliability data are needed
     b) It provides an overview of language strengths and
        weaknesses
     c) It can be used to help identify language-based learning
        disabilities
    *d) It can be used confidently for eligibility decisions

383. One approach that has been used to evaluate the spontaneous
     use of language in the natural setting is
    *a) language sampling
     b) whole language
     c) phonics
     d) structured interviews

384. The Tests of Language Development-3 includes measures of
    a) semantics only
    b) syntax only
  * c) semantics and syntax
    d) semantics and pragmatics

385. An analysis of a language sample should include which of the following?
    a) form
    b) content
    c) use
   *d) all of the above

386. The TOAL-3 is designed to measure
    a) receptive syntax
    b) expressive semantics
    c) receptive semantics
   *d) all of the above

TRUE-FALSE QUESTIONS

387. The Peabody Picture Vocabulary Test-III may be considered a valid measure of intelligence. F

388. The Test of Language Competence is based on research suggesting that children with language/learning disabilities have cognitive and linguistic deficits. T

389. The Tests of Language Development-3 provide a profile of a child's strengths and weaknesses in a variety of language areas using the same comparison group. T

390. The Peabody Picture Vocabulary Test-III was co-normed with the Expressive Vocabulary Test. T

391. The Language Processing Test-Revised can be used with students who experience seemingly poor memory, word-retrieval problems and nonspecific word usage. T

392. The Test of Pragmatic Skills can be used to assess semantic and/or syntax problems in addition to assessing language for conversational intent. F

393. The Test of Problem Solving-Revised requires verbal expression. T

394. The Test of Word Finding includes information for identifying types of word-finding skills in children. T

80

395. The Test of Adolescent and Adult Language-3 has been criticized because of the small number of subtests that measure many of the areas. T

396. Parts of the Test of Adolescent and Adult Language-3 can be group administered. T

397. The assessment of pragmatics focuses on the student's use of grammar and sentence structure. F

398. There has been a decreased emphasis on evaluating language in the natural environment over the past 40 years. F

399. Language sampling is a two step process that involves eliciting and recording a person's oral language in a natural setting. F

400. The TOAL-3 includes norms for young adults aged 18-24 enrolled in postsecondary programs. T

401. Similar to the PPVT-III, the CREVT uses black and white line drawings for the receptive language items. F

402. The primary function of language is communication. T

403. The Test of Word Finding is designed to measure the word finding ability of secondary school-aged children. F

OPEN-ENDED QUESTIONS OR DISCUSSION TOPICS

404. Explain what is meant by the term "pragmatics" in language. Why do you think the area of pragmatics has received a lot of attention in recent years?

405. How do you explain the popularity of the Peabody Picture Vocabulary Test-III? Discuss the most appropriate use of this test.

Item #	Page #	Item #	Page #
369.	251	387.	388
370.	251	388.	259
371.	243	389.	261
372.	244	390.	253
373.	257	391.	262
374.	262	392.	263
375.	243	393.	263
376.	256	394.	264

377.	259	395.	256,257
378.	247	396.	256
379.	249	397.	244
380.	262	398.	244
381.	243,244	399.	245
382.	250	400.	254
383.	245	401.	247
384.	259	402.	242
385.	246	403.	263
386.	254		

Chapter 12

Assessment of General Achievement

OVERVIEW AND TEACHING SUGGESTIONS

Achievement tests are perhaps the most widely used assessment instruments in schools. These test can be categorized into two groups: norm-referenced and criterion-referenced. Norm-referenced and criterion-referenced achievement tests can be subcategorized based upon the type of administration. Individually administered achievement tests are sometimes used to document results from group administered tests and/or to observe an individual's approach to academic tasks. Group tests are usually administered routinely to students several times during their "academic careers" to document levels of academic performance as well as progress in certain areas. Those group tests designed for the elementary grades usually emphasize the basic skill areas whereas those for older students emphasize content areas as well.

Inventories and criterion-referenced tests can be a great help to special educators. Typically, these instruments play an important role both in the informal assessment process (prereferral) and the IEP development in the formal process (postreferral). These instruments give specific information on what to teach and are often correlated with materials that can be used to facilitate that process. Most of these instruments are extremely comprehensive; usually only portions are administered. You must make sure that the areas covered in a particular instrument are the same as the goals/objectives that you are interested in teaching. Similarly, you must make sure that you agree with the standard of performance (criteria) established by the authors of criterion-referenced tests.

Although not officially considered screening tests, many achievement instruments actually fall into this category. They are often used as preliminary tests before a more comprehensive academic diagnostic assessment is conducted. The following topics/issues should be emphasized in this chapter:

*the important issue of content validity of achievement tests.

*limitations of most achievement tests with respect to obtaining specific teaching information

*the importance of error analysis in interpreting test results

*the advantages and disadvantages of using each individually administered achievement test

*the importance of choosing an instrument that is appropriate for the student being assessed

*the importance of choosing relevant portions of criterion-referenced instruments being administered

*the advantages and disadvantages of using criterion-referenced instruments

ACTIVITIES

12-1 ADMINISTRATION OF AN ACHIEVEMENT TEST

Purpose - To give students practice in administering, scoring,
and interpreting an achievement test.
Description - Provide students with testing permission slips to
be completed by parents of a child to be tested before tests are
administered. Each student should find an examine and administer
the WRAT-3. They should score the tests and report the
appropriate data. The instructor should double check all
scoring. Students should then analyze the errors made on the
test to obtain more information. A discussion should follow
focusing on 1) general problems in administration and scoring; 2)
the advantage and disadvantage of the WRAT-3 compared to error
analysis of classroom work products; and 3) the limitations of
the test regarding the areas that it measures.

12-2 DETERMINATION OF BASAL AND CEILING

Purpose - To give students practice in establishing basals and
ceilings of a test.
Description - After a lecture, the students should be asked to
determine the basal item and the ceiling item for the PIAT-R data
found in Exhibit 12-2. In addition, they should indicate the raw
score and which items were administered unnecessarily. A general
discussion of the advantages and disadvantages of basals and
ceilings should follow, including the issue of whether to "count"
the items that were administered unnecessarily (i.e. 39 in DATA 1
and 43 in DATA 2).

Answers:
DATA 1 basal item 41   DATA 2 basal item 25
       ceiling item 52   ceiling item 42
       raw score 47   raw score 34
       unnecessary items 38,40-53 unnecessary items 24,43-45

MULTIPLE CHOICE QUESTIONS

406. What is the most appropriate score to report on the WRAT-3
     for comparison purposes?
     a) stanine   c) percentile
    *b) standard score   d) grade equivalent

407. The most important type of validity for achievement tests is
     a) predictive   c) construct
    *b) content   d) concurrent

408. The Peabody Individual Achievement Test-Revised
    a) does not test written expression
    *b) is suitable for most individuals with speech/language and
       motor impairments
    c) has very high predictive validity
    d) can also be group administered

409. Which one of the following is not a group achievement test?
    a) California Achievement Tests
    b) Iowa Test of Basic Skills
    *c) Wide Range Achievement Test - 3
    d) SRA Achievement Series

410. The Wide Range Achievement Test-3 provides
    a) scores for reading comprehension and spelling
    b) scores for arithmetic, reading recognition, and reading
       comprehension
    c) scores for content areas including math, science, and
       social studies
    *d) scores for spelling, arithmetic, and reading

411. Which instrument includes a locater test to identify which
    level to use with a particular student ?
    a) Stanford Achievement Tests
    b) Tests of Achievement and Proficiency
    c) Iowa Test of Basic Skills
    *d) California Achievement Tests

412. The subtest on the PIAT-R that does not involve visual input
    is
    a) reading recognition   c) reading comprehension
    b) spelling   *d) general information

413. The reading subtest on the WRAT-3 is similar to the
    _____ subtest from the PIAT-R
    *a) reading recognition   c) spelling
    b) reading comprehension   d) general information

414. Which of the following does not describe the BASIS?
    a) Is primarily a screening instrument
    b) Uses cloze procedure to measure reading
    c) Covers the areas of math, reading, spelling, writing
    *d) Is designed for preschool children

415. The K-TEA provides
    a) individual subtest scores and battery composite score
    b) error analysis guidelines
    c) test items similar to classroom demands
    *d) all of the above

416. The most relevant information obtained from the Brigance
     Inventory of Essential Skills (red) is
     *a) behavioral objectives that focus on "functional
         academics"
     b) IQ and specific subtest scores
     c) academic or estimated learning potential
     d) a prediction of kindergarten success

417. Which of the following is true of the Multilevel Academic
     Survey Test?
     a) it does not go below 1st grade level
     *b) it has grade level and curriculum level tests
     c) it is norm-referenced only
     d) it is criterion-referenced only

418. Some research on the K-TEA suggests that it
     a) yields lower scores than other achievement tests
     *b) yields higher scores than other achievement tests
     c) yields very similar scores as other achievement tests
     d) cannot be compared with other achievement tests

419. The Brigance Inventory of Basic Skills (blue) measures
     a) developmental skills
     b) secondary level academic skills
     *c) readiness and academic skills through grade six
     d) adaptive behavior skills

420. The Wechsler Individual Achievement Test
     a) does not include a measure of reading comprehension
     b) can be used with secondary-level students
     *c) does not include a measure of general information
     d) does not require any writing

421. A common criticism of the WRAT-3 is
     a) its difficulty of administration
     *b) its lack of a reading comprehension component
     c) its cost
     d) its lack of reliability

TRUE-FALSE QUESTIONS

422. The PIAT-R would be a good test to use with a student with a
     visual problem. F

423. The WIAT has a linking sample with the Stanford-Binet-4. F

424. The WRAT-3 includes a measure of written arithmetic
     computation. F

425. In general, individual achievement tests are administered more frequently than group achievement tests to the school population. F

426. It is best to use the composite scores of the Diagnostic Achievement Battery-2 rather than the subtest scores for educational decisions. T

427. The WIAT has subtests that correspond to the IDEA definition of learning disabilities. T

428. The BASIS provides criterion-referenced as well as norm-referenced information about students. T

429. There are available sets of tables to allow a comparison of IQs with scores from the Norris Educational Achievement Test. T

430. The K-TEA is in an easy-to-administer easel format. T

431. The Comprehensive Inventory of Basic Skills-Revised (green) is the Brigance Inventory of choice for older elementary and younger secondary students. T

432. The Brigance Inventory of Essential Skills (red) includes a computer scoring system. F

433. The DATA-2 is the only individually administered achievement test designed specifically for adolescents. T

434. The use of individual subtest scores on the DATA-2 is recommended due to its high content validity. F

435. The DATA-2 can best be described as a criterion-referenced achievement test. F

436. Some research indicates that the K-TEA yields higher scores than other achievement tests. T

437. Although primarily used as a criterion-referenced measure, the Brigance Comprehensive Inventory of basic Skills (green) also provides norm-referenced scores. T

438. The Mini-Battery of Achievement is actually a shorter version of the Wechsler Individual Achievement Test F

439. The Hammill Multiability Achievement Test is co-normed with an intelligence test to provide IQ/achievement comparisons using the same standardization sample. T

440. The reliability of the composite scores from the Diagnostic Achievement Battery-2 is higher than the reliability of the individual subtest scores. T

OPEN-ENDED QUESTIONS OR DISCUSSION TOPICS

441. In relation to the various learning-related disabilities, what are the considerations in determining whether the PIAT-R or a more traditional achievement measure should be used to assess academic achievement?

442. What are the advantages of an individual achievement test, compared to a group achievement test?

443. Why shouldn't you use WRAT-3 grade equivalent scores to judge the effectiveness of a teaching approach?

444. How would you decide which individual achievement measure to choose to help determine IEP goals for a child? Tell what characteristics of the child and test would influence your decision.

445. What are the advantages of inventories and criterion-referenced tests compared to norm-referenced achievement tests?

446. How would you determine which skill sequences you would administer if you were to test a student with the Brigance Inventory of Basic Skills (blue)?

Item #	Page #	Item #	Page #
406.	294	424.	293
407.	270	425.	269
408.	287	426.	278
409.	293	427.	290
410.	293	428.	297
411.	271	429.	298
412.	287	430.	282
413.	287,293	431.	306
414.	296	432.	305
415.	283,286	433.	282
416.	302	434.	282
417.	306	435.	278
418.	285	436.	286
419.	299	437.	305
420.	290,291	438.	299

421.	296	439.	297
422.	289	440.	278
423.	293		

Exhibit 12-2

Given the following data from two presentations of the PIAT-R,
answer the following questions.

a. What is the basal item?
b. What is the ceiling item?
c. What items were administered unnecessarily?
d. What is the raw score?

DATA SET 1   38. C   46. I
                    39. I   47. C
                    40. C   48. I
                    41. C   49. I
                    42. C   50. C
                    43. C   51. I
started here-->44. C   52. I
                    45. C   53. I

                A._____   B._____
                C._____   D._____

DATA SET 2   24. C   35. C
                    25. C   36. I
                    26. C   37. C
                    27. C   38. I
                    28. C   39. I
                    29. C   40. C
                    30. I   41. I
                    31. C   42. I
                    32. I   43. C
started here-->33. C   44. I
                    34. I   45. I

                A._____   B._____
                C._____   D._____

C = Correct response
I = Incorrect response

Chapter 13

Assessment of Reading

OVERVIEW AND TEACHING SUGGESTIONS

Much attention has been paid to the assessment of reading skills due to the relationship of an individual's skills in reading and his/her school success. Reading skills are not only needed for success in the school environment, but also in the home and community environments. Given these relationships, it is of vital importance to accurately assess a students' skills to provide them with the necessary instruction to become "good" readers.

The assessment of reading is a complex task. There are a myriad of theoretical models suggesting a wide array of skills necessary for a student to be successful in the area reading. The model of Ekwall and Shankar (1988), however, offers a cohesive framework for the components of reading and its subsequent assessment. There is also growing evidence for the increased need of informal assessment of reading skills. This could include the use of informal reading inventories and portfolio assessment (discussed in Chapter 7) among others. The following topics should be emphasized:

        *the components of reading

        *advantages and disadvantages of using informal reading
         inventories

*diagnostic reading tests are not "diagnostic" in the
traditional sense

*the advantages and disadvantages of using formal and
informal methods to assess the reading skills of
children

ACTIVITIES

13-1 SCORING OF A STANDARDIZED READING TEST

Purpose - To give students practice in using a variety of tables
to convert raw scores to derived scores.
Description - Using the following raw scores from the TORC-3,
have students convert them to scaled scores and the R.C.Q.
(provide TORC-3 manual). Discussion could focus on how a low raw
score on a particular subtest could result in a relatively high
scaled score.

TORC-3 SCORES

Subtest	RS	SS
GV	5	10
SynSim	7	13
PR	2	8
MV	3	11
SSV	2	8
SV	5	12
RD	1	5
SS	7	9

R.C.Q. = 102

Note:
Student is 7 years, 8 months old

13-2 ADMINISTRATION OF AN INFORMAL READING INVENTORY

Purpose - To provide the student with an opportunity to evaluate a child's reading level using an Informal Reading Inventory.
Description - Students are furnished with an IRI (such as the Ekwall) and instructed to administer the instrument to an elementary school child. Next, each student will be required to write a brief report, indicating the child's independent, instructional and frustration reading levels, focusing on an error analysis.

MULTIPLE-CHOICE QUESTIONS

447. The Woodcock Reading Mastery Tests-Revised
     a) are group administered
     b) are informal criterion-referenced instruments
     c) are best suited for high school students
    *d) include a test of word attack skills

448. The Stanford Diagnostic Reading Test-4
     a) was designed to assess the reading ability of young children with mild disabilities
     b) utilizes an "easel" format for ease in administration
     c) is not norm referenced
    *d) is a group reading test for grades 1 through 12

449. The Diagnostic Reading Scales
     a) is a group reading test
     b) measures reading comprehension only
    *c) contains a section on administrative considerations for non-standard English speaking children
     d) was designed to assess the reading ability of young children with mild disabilities

450. Which one of the following utilizes a modified "cloze" procedure to assess paragraph comprehension?
    *a) Woodcock Reading Mastery Tests-Revised
     b) Stanford Diagnostic Reading Tests
     c) Gray Oral Reading Test-3
     d) Durrell Analysis of Reading Difficulty

451. The Durrell Analysis of Reading Difficulty
    *a) provides check lists to identify deficient areas in reading
     b) is a group reading test
     c) utilizes a "maze" procedure to assess reading comprehension
     d) assesses only the ability to orally read/decode words

452. One advantage of the Stanford Diagnostic Reading Test-4 is that
    a) it focuses on oral reading
  *b) it can be group administered
    c) it provides an error analysis
    d) it focuses on prereading skills

453. Which of the following is true of the Test of Reading Comprehension-3?
    a) it is only individually administered
    b) it assesses oral reading skills
    c) it should not be used for those with articulation problems
  *d) it assesses silent reading comprehension

454. The _____ includes a Relative Performance Index that indicates relative mastery of content at a specific grade level or age level.
    a) Stanford Diagnostic Reading Test-4
    b) Durrell Analysis of Reading Difficulty
  *c) Woodcock Reading Mastery Tests-Revised
    d) Test of Reading Comprehension-3

455. The most widely accepted criteria for the independent, instructional, and frustration reading levels are those proposed by
    a) Ekwall
  *b) Betts
    c) Brigance
    d) Fuller

456. Which of the following is group-administered?
    a) Gray Oral Reading Test-Diagnostic
  *b) Stanford Diagnostic Reading Test-4
    c) Test of Reading Comprehension-3
    d) Woodcock Reading Mastery Tests-Revised

457. Informal reading inventories are typically used to determine what three levels of reading proficiency?
    a) leisure, academic, frustration
    b) independent, dependent, functional
  *c) independent, instructional, frustration
    d) failure, instructional, success

458. Which of the following is/are major component(s) of the reading process?
   a) recognition
   b) analysis
   c) comprehension
   *d) all of the above

459. The immediate identification of a word by a reader even though the reader might not understand its meaning is known as
   *a) sight word identification
   b) word analysis
   c) word attack
   d) oral reading vocabulary

460. The main subcomponents of word recognition are
   *a) sight word identification and word analysis
   b) word analysis and word attack
   c) sight word identification and word attack
   d) none of the above

461. Which of the following statements is not true about the Woodcock Diagnostic Reading Battery?
   a) It includes subtests from the Woodcock-Johnson-Revised
   b) It measures reading achievement and reading aptitude
   *c) It includes measures from the Diagnostic Achievement Battery-2
   d) It includes both cognitive and achievement subtests

462. An informal procedure that is very helpful in determining instructional strategies is
   *a) error analysis
   b) video taping
   c) audio taping
   d) none of the above

463. Oral reading tests usually focus upon assessing skill(s) of
   a) literal comprehension
   b) word attack
   *c) reading speed and accuracy
   d) all of the above

TRUE-FALSE QUESTIONS

464. The names of the two most common tests of oral reading skills are the Gray and Gilmore. T

465. The word comprehension subtest of the Woodcock Reading Mastery Tests-Revised includes an analogy section. T

466. The Stanford Diagnostic Reading Test-4 is a group test that can be used to group students for instructional purposes. T

467. The Test of Reading Comprehension-3 also measures vocabulary and syntax. T

468. Informal reading inventories typically include graded passages to measure word recognition and comprehension. T

469. Commercially prepared informal reading inventories have been criticized for lack of reliability and validity. T

470. Informal reading inventories are less prone to measurement errors than standardized reading tests. F

471. The importance of reading in relationship to school success is minimal because students are frequently lectured. F

472. The evaluation of the reading process should only be conducted utilizing formal procedures/techniques. F

473. An advantage of assessing the reading process informally is the opportunity to understand the reading process rather than simply to analyze the reading product. T

474. More formal tests of reading are often referred to as diagnostic reading tests. T

475. Most oral reading tests focus on the areas of reading speed and accuracy. T

476. The cloze procedure requires the use of a computer. F

477. The cloze procedure is similar to the maze procedure, except that vertically presented choices are used in the cloze procedure instead of blanks. F

478. The Reading Diagnosis Sheet is an informal procedure for reading evaluation that breaks down the reading process into 28 areas. T

479. The "think-aloud" procedure involves having a student read a passage (a sentence or a clause at a time) and tell what he or she is thinking about or what might happen next. T

480. The GORT-D includes a large number of structural reading tasks. T

481. The GORT-D is a diagnostic reading test that includes primarily traditional reading tasks. F

OPEN-ENDED QUESTIONS OR DISCUSSION TOPICS

482. What factors should be taken into consideration when selecting a diagnostic reading test? Your response should include type(s) of reading difficulty and intended use of specific diagnostic reading tests.

Item #	Page #	Item #	Page #
447.	327	465.	327
448.	321	466.	321
449.	331	467.	326
450.	327	468.	313
451.	331	469.	314
452.	321	470.	313
453.	324	471.	310
454.	327	472.	312
455.	313	473.	312
456.	321	474.	312
457.	313	475.	312
458.	310	476.	315,316
459.	311	477.	315
460.	310,311	478.	317
461.	331	479.	317
462.	316	480.	321
463.	312	481.	321
464.	332		

Chapter 14

Assessment of Mathematics

OVERVIEW AND TEACHING SUGGESTIONS

Although given less attention than the assessment of reading, the assessment of mathematics is also a vital component of any comprehensive basic skill assessment. A detailed examination of the general achievement tests described in Chapter 12 indicates that math subtests exist in almost every instrument. Assessment in the area of mathematics will usually include a measure of student performance in the areas of math concepts, computation, application, and problem-solving. Norm-referenced tests in the various areas of mathematics are often referred to as diagnostic tests that determine areas of strength and weakness; diagnostic math tests pinpoint areas for remediation rather than "diagnosing" in the traditional sense.

Criterion-referenced tests in this area are used to provide specific information about the math skills that the student does and does not have. These tests are used more to develop specific educational programs. The following issues/topics should be emphasized when presenting this chapter:

　　*the importance of assessment in the area of math as part

　　　of a comprehensive assessment of basic skills

　　*strengths and limitations of norm- and criterion-

　　　referenced tests to aid in the assessment of math

　　*the importance of the use of error analysis when

conducting assessments in the area of math

<u>ACTIVITY</u>

14-1 DETERMINATION OF AREAS TO BE MEASURED

<u>Purpose</u> - To provide the student with the experience in determining the most appropriate instrument(s) and areas to administer.
<u>Description</u> - Provide the class with a description of a student (see Exhibit 14-1). Each individual should analyze the description to determine the specific areas that need further evaluation. Next, the students should critique the various inventories and CRTs (including those discussed in Chapter 13) to determine the most appropriate instrument. Finally, the specific relevant sections of the chosen instruments should be identified.

<u>MULTIPLE CHOICE QUESTIONS</u>

483. Which one of the following is <u>not</u> true of the KeyMath - Revised?
    a) it utilizes an "easel" format for ease in administration
    *b) it is primarily a paper-pencil test
    c) it has strong evidence for its validity
    d) it is best used informally as a criterion-referenced test

484. The TOMA-2 includes a subtest on
    a) teacher ratings of math
    b) math interests
    *c) attitude toward math
    d) advanced mathematical operations

485. The _____ includes measures of math applications such as telling time.
    *a) KeyMath-Revised
    b) Test of Mathematical Abilities-2
    c) Stanford Diagnostic Mathematics Test-4
    d) none of the above

486. The Stanford Diagnostic Mathematics Test-4 should be mainly used for
    a) determining instructional objectives
    b) classifying students
    c) determining the math curriculum to use
    *d) comparing students' math performances and identifying general strengths and weaknesses

487. The Test of Mathematical Abilities-2 does not measure
    a) math-related vocabulary
    b) knowledge of general math information
    c) paper-and-pencil computation
   *d) computer-related math

488. An informal technique for assessing math skills that
    combines error analysis and curriculum-based assessment is
    referred to by the mnemonic
    *a) APPLY   c) MATH
    b) TEACH   d) PROBE

489. The _____ is associated with a
    comprehensive program called Project Math
    a) Enright Inventory of Basic Arithmetic Skills
    b) KeyMath - Revised
    c) Brigance Inventory of Essential Skills
   *d) Mathematics Concept Inventory

490. One of the advantages of the SDMT-4 is that
    a) it focuses on computer skills
    b) it provides an error analysis
   *c) it can be group administered
    d) it focuses on prearithmetic skills

491. The interpretation of the Enright Inventory of Basic
    Arithmetic Skills should include
    *a) an error analysis of the computation problems
    b) determination of the grade equivalents yielded by the
       instrument
    c) a careful analysis of the percentile ranks
    d) analysis of the math concepts demonstrated by the student

492. The Diagnostic Test of Arithmetic Strategies
    a) is a norm-referenced instrument
    b) provides information on what basic number facts a student
       has
   *c) provides information on how a student performs math
       problems
    d) none of the above

493. Computation involves which of the following areas?
    a) subtraction of decimals
    b) addition of fractions
    c) multiplication of whole numbers
   *d) all of the above

494. Enright, Gable, and Hendrickson developed a nine-step model for which approach to math assessment?
   a) oral examination
   b) diagnostic analysis
   *c) error analysis
   d) interviewing

495. The KeyMath-Revised is a potentially useful instrument for students identified as having
   a) mental retardation
   b) an emotional problem
   *c) a learning disability
   d) all of the above

TRUE-FALSE QUESTIONS

496. Parts of the Test of Mathematical Abilities-2 may not be appropriate for children with certain disabilities and should be eliminated from their assessments. T

497. The KeyMath-Revised measures the major areas of content and operations although no application items are included. F

498. The KeyMath-Revised is better used as a screening instrument than a diagnostic test for students with mental retardation. T

499. The Stanford Diagnostic Mathematics Test-4 can be group administered. T

500. The TOMA-2 may be either individually or group administered. T

501. The TOMA-2 provides only standard scores. F

502. The Enright Inventory of Basic Arithmetic Skills should not be used to develop IEP objectives. F

503. The Stanford Diagnostic Mathematics Test-4 is primarily a test of written math calculation. F

504. The Diagnostic Test of Arithmetic Strategies measures the procedures that students use when they solve computation problems. T

505. The Mathematics Concept Inventory should be used to monitor progress toward IEP objectives. T

506. The Enright Inventory of Basic Arithmetic Skills sets a criterion level of 95% accuracy for computational skills. F

507. The Enright Inventory of Basic Arithmetic Skills is not designed for high school students. T

508. Norm-referenced tests for the math areas are sometimes referred to as diagnostic tests. T

509. For mathematics assessment, it is important to use error analysis procedures.

510. Problem-solving includes such components as money skills and time concepts. F

511. The DTAS is based on an error analysis approach. F

512. The Test of Mathematical Abilities-2 includes a subtest on attitude toward math. T

513. The DTAS requires a student to describe how they are solving mathematical problems. T

514. As compared to the area of reading, less attention is given to the assessment of math. T

515. Math is not really a significant area of concern when conducting a comprehensive basic skill assessment. F

516. The Stanford Diagnostic Mathematics Tests-4 are available for several age/grade levels. T

517. The Chronometric Analysis of Math Strategies is a computerized test that measures response latencies of a student solving computation problems. T

OPEN-ENDED QUESTIONS OR DISCUSSION TOPICS

518. Discuss how the results of the KeyMath-Revised can best be used in the development of a child's IEP.

Item #	Page #	Item #	Page #
483.	337,340	501.	344
484.	344	502.	350
485.	338	503.	341
486.	343	504.	345
487.	343,344	505.	352

488.	354	506.	350
489.	352	507.	347
490.	340,343	508.	337
491.	350	509.	353
492.	346	510.	336,337
493.	336	511.	345,346
494.	353	512.	344
495.	340	513.	346
496.	345	514.	336
497.	337	515.	336
498.	340	516.	340,341
499.	340,343	517.	354
500.	343		

Exhibit 14-1

Albert is a fourth grade student who has always been "scared of numbers." He often confuses the mathematics signs and will add instead of subtract or subtract instead of divide. He also has great difficulty in time and number concepts. He still has problems reading and understanding a clock. Albert's teacher felt that a sequential list of objectives in the deficient math areas would be very beneficial. He was referred for testing to evaluate his overall mathematics ability and to identify appropriate educational objectives.

Chapter 15

Assessment of Written Expression

Other than speaking, the primary form of expression for most individuals is writing. Written expression is also a necessary requirement for school success. Written expression is actually comprised of several components. These are handwriting, spelling, mechanics, usage, and ideation. Mechanics refers to the rules of writing such as capitalization and punctuation. Usage refers to how the various areas of written language are chosen and combined. Ideation relates to the use of written ideas to meet the writer's purpose and intent. For example, written expression would take a different form when it is used for a personal letter or for a take-home exam.

The evaluation of written expression can be both formal and informal. Norm-referenced tests are available to measure the overall area of written language and major components such as spelling. Informal assessment is often conducted by an analysis of a writing sample, a procedure that is analogous to language sampling discussed in Chapter 11. The following major points should be addressed in this chapter:

*the importance of assessing written expression

*the various components of written expression

*the strengths and limitations of specific written expression tests

*the strengths and limitations of diagnostic spelling tests

*the importance of informal assessment

*how to conduct an error analysis of writing products

ACTIVITIES

15-1 ADMINISTRATION AND SCORING OF A NORM-REFERENCED TEST OF WRITTEN EXPRESSION

Purpose - To provide the student with an opportunity to administer and score a test of written language and determine the strengths and limitations of this type of assessment.
Description - Students should have access to either the TOWE or the TOWL-3. Instruct students to select a volunteer of the appropriate age for the test and administer the TOWE/TOWL-3. After scoring, students can prepare a short report that includes results and interpretation. In-class discussion can focus on any problems in scoring the writing sample portion of the tests.

15-2 ANALYZING A WRITING SAMPLE

Purpose - To give the students practice in informally analyzing a spontaneous writing sample.
Description - Have each student collect two samples of writing from an elementary student. Using the guidelines found in Figure 15-4 in the chapter, an informal analysis should be conducted. Students should look for similarities in the samples as well as differences based on the intent of the writing task (ideation).

MULTIPLE CHOICE QUESTIONS

519. The component of written language that has to do with the rules such as punctuation is
    a) spelling
    *b) mechanics
    c) usage
    d) ideation

520. Which component of written language is concerned with the writer's intent?
    a) spelling
    b) mechanics
    c) usage
    *d) ideation

521. The Test of Written Expression includes a writing sample called the
    a) product
    b) sample
    c) example
    *d) essay

522. The Test of Written Expression measures which of these areas?
    a) mechanics
    b) usage
    c) ideation
    *d) all of the above

523. The Test of Written Language-3 measures
    a) spontaneous language only
    b) contrived language only
    c) written language of adults
    *d) spontaneous and contrived language

524. Which of the following is not true about the Written scales of the OWLS?
    a) It measures Conventions, Linguistics, and Content
    *b) It uses basals and ceilings
    c) It includes direct and indirect writing tasks
    d) It can be administered to small groups

525. Which of the following is not true of the Test of Early Written Language?
    a) it focuses on emerging written language skills
    b) it includes measures of creative expression and record keeping
    *c) it can be used confidently with children as young as 3 years
    d) its validity has been questioned

526. The Written Language Assessment
    a) is a criterion-referenced test
    *b) uses writing samples
    c) requires the student to copy a paragraph
    d) none of the above

527. The Test of Written Spelling-3 includes two word lists called
    a) preprimer and primer
    b) easy and difficult
    c) homonyms and synonyms
    *d) predictable and unpredictable

528. Which of the following is <u>not</u> true of the TWS-3?
    a) it has two word lists
    *b) error analysis should not be used
    c) it can be group administered
    d) there are guidelines to indicate when testing is
       discontinued

529. Which one of the following is <u>not</u> a part of Spellmaster
    a) diagnostic tests
    b) irregular word tests
    *c) survey tests
    d) homonym tests

530. The Spellmaster
    a) is a criterion-referenced test
    b) emphasizes error analysis
    c) can be used to help group students
    *d) all of the above

531. Which one of the following instruments is comprised of 100
    spelling words categorized as predictable and unpredictable?
    a) Spellmaster
    *b) TWS-3
    c) both a & b
    d) neither a or b

532. According to Luts (1991) the most common written expression
    error is
    *a) spelling
    b) punctuation
    c) capitalization
    d) grammar

533. The Writing Process Test requires the student to
    a) write about anything
    *b) plan and write an article for an intended audience
    c) react to a photograph
    d) to write a paragraph about "my favorite hobby"

534. "John threw the ball to me and I threw it back" has how many
    thought units?
    a) 0
    b) 1
    *c) 2
    d) 11

535. The Computerized Test of Spelling Errors
    a) can be used to score results from the TWS-3
    b) is part of the Spellmaster system
    *c) analyzes errors of 40 spelling words
    d) none of the above

TRUE-FALSE QUESTIONS

536. Handwriting is not considered a component of written language. F

537. Mechanics refers to the rules of written language (e.g., capitalization and punctuation). T

538. Ideation refers to the degree of creativity in written expression. F

539. The Test of Written Expression has two sections- the items and the essay. T

540. In the Test of Written Expression, the same item might be used to measure more than one component of written language. T

541. The Test of Written Language-3 uses pictures as the stimulus items to generate the spontaneous writing sample. T

542. The TOWL-3 includes a subtest that measures spelling. T

543. The Test of Written English is a criterion-referenced test. T

544. The Test of Early Written Language can be used confidently with children as young as age 3. F

545. One advantage of the Written Language Assessment is that it uses real writing tasks in a natural setting. T

546. Error analysis should be used with the TWS-3 to provide additional information. T

547. The Written scales from the OWLS measure writing fluency but not mechanics. F

548. The Spellmaster can aid in determining groups for spelling instruction. T

549. The diagnostic test of the Spellmaster includes words that violate basic phonics rules. F

550. The interpretation of the Spellmaster should focus on the standard scores that are yielded. F

551. The Mather-Woodcock Group Writing Tests can only be scored using a computer program. T

552. Errors of style include errors in such areas as grammar, mechanics, and diction. T

553. A thought unit is always a complete sentence. F

OPEN-ENDED QUESTIONS OR DISCUSSION TOPICS

554. What are the components of written language? What role does each play in the area of written expression?

555. Describe how you would conduct an informal evaluation of a writing sample.

Item #	Page #	Item #	Page #
519.	359	537.	359
520.	359	538.	359
521.	363	539.	362
522.	365	540.	362
523.	365	541.	366
524.	361	542.	366
525.	370	543.	371
526.	371	544.	370
527.	371	545.	371
528.	373	546.	373
529.	373	547.	362
530.	373,375	548.	373
531.	371	549.	373
532.	378	550.	373
533.	370	551.	369
534.	375	552.	375
535.	378	553.	375
536.	359		

Chapter 16

Comprehensive Assessment Systems

Some norm-referenced instruments include several components and are sometimes referred to as assessment systems. In some cases, more than one area is measured. For example, measures of both cognition and achievement might be included. Examples of this type of assessment system are the Differential Ability Scales, the Kaufman Assessment Battery for Children, and the Woodcock-Johnson-Revised. These instruments have the advantage of allowing comparisons of IQ and achievement with the same standardization sample. This is particularly important when making eligibility decisions that require such comparisons.

Other assessment systems provide multiple measures of the same area. These typically allow a comprehensive, ecological assessment of an individual's behavior. For example, a student's behavior might be rated by parents and teachers, and allow for a self-rating as well. The Behavior Assessment System for Children and the Social Skills Rating System are two examples of this type of comprehensive Assessment System. The following issues/topics should be emphasized in this chapter:

* the importance of cognitive/achievement assessment systems and their role in helping to make eligibility decisions

* the importance of behavior assessment systems in

                    providing an ecological assessment

             * the strengths and limitations of the various

                assessment systems

ACTIVITIES

16-1 COMPARING INSTRUMENT TO THEORY

Purpose - To allow students to see how intelligence test items
are developed using a theoretical base.
Description - Have the students research the Horn-Cattell theory
of intelligence, then provide a copy of the Woodcock-Johnson-
Revised Cognitive Battery (Standard and Supplemental). They
should determine how the constructs measured by the WJ-R are
similar to or different from those included in the model.

16-2 INTERVIEW ABOUT SOCIAL SKILLS

Purpose - To give students the opportunity to determine teachers'
perceptions of social skills.
Description - Have the students interview both general education
and special education teachers at different grade levels. Items
on the Social Skills Rating System can be compared with the
teachers' views to determine if it reflects their perceptions.

MULTIPLE CHOICE QUESTIONS

556. The Kaufman Assessment Battery for Children
      a) measures only verbal intelligence
     *b) measures simultaneous and sequential processing skills
      c) measures interests and achievement
      d) measures primarily fine-motor skills

557. Research has shown that the Kaufman Assessment Battery for
     Children has questionable
      a) criterion-related validity
     *b) construct validity
      c) use with older elementary school children
      d) use with children without disabilities

558. One of the many features of the Woodcock-Johnson-Revised is
      a) good standardization
      b) continuous-year norms
      c) computer scoring
     *d) all of the above

559. Simultaneous processing as measured by the K-ABC requires an individual to
    a) arrange stimuli in serial order
    b) demonstrate math and reading ability simultaneously
    c) simultaneously process visual and verbal stimuli
    *d) integrate and synthesize spatial or analogic information

560. Which of the following is not true of the Differential Ability Scales?
    a) It is a battery of cognitive and achievement tests
    b) It has two levels- preschool and school-aged
    *c) It has good reliability but poor validity
    d) It is an updated version of the British Ability Scales

561. Which of the following is not true about cognitive / achievement systems?
    a) Can be used to establish IEP goals
    b) Can be helpful in identifying individuals with learning disabilities
    *c) Are typically administered by teachers
    d) Are typically administered by school psychologists

562. Which of the following type of measure is not included in the achievement section of the Differential Ability Scales?
    a) math calculation
    *b) math concepts
    c) written spelling
    d) oral reading

563. The cognitive section of the Woodcock-Johnson-Revised is based on which theory?
    a) Gardner's multiple intelligence
    *b) Horn-Cattell
    c) Das-Luria
    d) None of the above

564. The RMI from the Woodcock-Johnson-Revised is expressed as
    a) a fraction whose numerator is always 10
    *b) a fraction whose denominator is always 90
    c) a percentile rank
    d) a standard score with a mean of 50

565. The Behavior Assessment System for Children includes all of these components except a
    a) teacher rating scale
    b) parent rating scale
    *c) peer rating scale
    d) self-report of personality

566. The Social Skills Rating System possesses several positive
     characteristics including which of the following?
     a) an associated curriculum
    *b) an assessment-intervention record
     c) a computer scoring system
     d) none of the above

567. The Teacher Rating Scales from the Behavior Assessment
     System for Children includes items that measure areas called
     a) adaptive and maladaptive problems
     b) positive and negative behaviors
     c) typical and atypical behaviors
    *d) internalizing and externalizing problems

568. The Student Observation System from the Behavior Assessment
     System for Children uses
    *a) momentary time sampling
     b) duration recording
     c) event recording
     d) interval recording

569. Which of the following is not true about the Social Skills
     Rating System?
     a) includes a preschool, elementary, and secondary level
     b) includes a teacher, parent, and student form
    *c) includes a measure of adaptive skills
     d) includes a measure of academic competence

570. Which of the following is true regarding the preschool
     version of the SSRS?
    *a) It is limited because of a small standardization sample
     b) The preschool version is not standardized
     c) It has excellent validity
     d) There is no preschool version

571. Intellectual ability as measured by the K-ABC
     a) is based on the Horn-Cattell model
     b) is based on Gardner's multiple intelligence theory
    *c) is based on cognitive and neuropsychology
     d) does not really have a theoretical base

TRUE - FALSE QUESTIONS

572. The K-ABC would be a good choice to use when testing a child
     with a vision impairment. F

573. There is a preschool version of the Differential Ability
     Scales. T

574. The theoretical framework of the cognitive section of the Woodcock-Johnson-Revised is based on the Horn-Cattell model. T

575. It is possible to compare an individual's scores on the Behavior Assessment System for Children using both clinical and normal groups. T

576. The Social Skills Rating System provides excellent diagnostic information but lacks linkage of that information to intervention strategies. F

577. Two advantages of the Behavior Assessment System for Children are the inclusion of a validity scale and separate scales for anxiety and depression. T

578. The preschool level of the Differential Ability Scales is further broken down into two sublevels. T

579. The Differential Ability Scales has a very comprehensive achievement section compared with other assessment systems. F

580. The K-ABC is very useful with gifted students and preschool children. F

581. The K-ABC can be used with both adolescents and adults. F

582. Scoring the Woodcock-Johnson-Revised is easy, requiring only one table. F

583. A Spanish version of the Woodcock-Johnson-Revised is available. T

584. Behavior assessment systems are typically administered to more than one individual. T

585. One component of the BASC is a structured developmental history. T

586. Two additional features of the BASC is a quick measure of ADHD and computer scoring. T

587. Unlike other behavior rating scales, the SSRS has no items focusing on problem behaviors. F

588. Some research indicates that mothers and fathers rate their child differently using the SSRS. T

OPEN-ENDED QUESTIONS OR DISCUSSION TOPICS

589. How would you defend the use of an ecological assessment, like the Behavior Assessment System for Children, when someone argues that it is too time-consuming?

590. Discuss the advantages and disadvantages of using a cognitive/achievement assessment system.

Item #	Page #	Item #	Page #
556.	389	573.	385
557.	394	574.	395
558.	400,401	575.	405
559.	389	576.	411,412
560.	385,389	577.	407
561.	384	578.	385
562.	386	579.	389
563.	395	580.	394
564.	398	581.	395
565.	401	582.	401
566.	411,412	583.	401
567.	402	584.	384
568.	405	585.	401
569.	408,409	586.	408
570.	412	587.	409
571.	389	588.	411
572.	394		

Chapter 17

Early Childhood Assessment

<u>OVERVIEW AND TEACHING SUGGESTIONS</u>

Legislative mandates, such as Public Law P.L. 99-457 have, in part, provided the impetus for increased interest in the area of early childhood assessment. The importance of a team approach in early childhood assessment must be emphasized. A number of guidelines have been presented by various educational agencies and professional organizations to assure the most accurate and beneficial information possible for the formulation of subsequent interventions.

The current chapter focuses on five specific areas of concern in the assessment of young children. Those areas include: (1) the importance of team assessment and play assessment, (2) developmental screening, (3) norm-referenced developmental testing, (4) preacademic testing, and (5) testing for educational programming. The following issues/topics should be emphasized in this chapter:

* the importance of a team approach

* the importance of a carefully planned evaluation of young children

* the importance of predictive validity of assessment instruments used with this population

* the applicability of other instruments to young children

ACTIVITIES

17-1 DETERMINING WHAT DEVELOPMENTAL ASSESSMENT PROCEDURES ARE CURRENTLY IN USE IN THE LOCAL AREA (FOR UNDERGRADUATE STUDENTS)

Purpose - To make students aware of what developmental-skills instruments are being used in their locale.
Description - Ask students to identify and interview three professionals who work with infants and toddlers with disabilities. One person should be from the local school system. The second should be associated with an agency (e.g. ARC or UCP). The third should be from the medical community. A comparison of the various procedures and a presentation of how they might be coordinated should be made.

17-2 CLASS DISCUSSION OF P.L. 99-457

Purpose - To familiarize students with the latest legislation affecting preschool disabled students and make them aware of the problems in implementation.
Description - Provide students with a copy of P.L. 99-457. As a take-home assignment, each student should review the law and be prepared to discuss the following issues: 1) How will school districts locate the appropriate children, birth to age five? 2) Once located, who will assess these children? 3) What instruments and procedures might be most valid with this population? 4) What problems might arise in the assessment of very young disabled children? 5) Should these children be labeled or should a noncategorical model be used?

591. The Callier-Azusa Scale
    *a) was specifically designed for individuals with sensory and motor deficits
    b) is best used to determine specific developmental levels of severely disabled children
    c) can be group administered
    d) measures only communication skills

592. The Brigance Inventory of Early Development- Revised (yellow)
    a) has excellent reliability and validity
    b) measures only reading readiness and basic math skills
    *c) should not be administered in its entirety
    d) does not provide information relevant for educational programming

593. Criterion-referenced developmental assessment instruments
     (e.g., the Brigance Inventory)
     a) provide valuable age equivalents
    *b) provide detailed skill sequences
     c) are most appropriate for older individuals
     d) do not provide information relevant for educational
        programming

594. Which procedure(s) is used to obtain information for the
     Battelle Developmental Inventory?
     a) interview and observation
     b) observation only
     c) traditional administration
    *d) interview, observation, and traditional administration

595. Which of the following is a norm-referenced test?
    *a) Denver II
     b) Callier-Azusa Scale
     c) Vulpe' Assessment Battery
     d) all of the above

596. The key piece of legislation that outlined specific
     responsibilities for the identification and
     appropriate educational programming for children from birth
     was
     a) P. L. 94-142
     b) P.L. 101-476
    *c) P.L. 99-457
     d) none of the above

597. One of the primary responsibilities of the teacher as a
     member of the interdisciplinary team is to
    *a) help coordinate assessment results
     b) act as the team leader
     c) keep accurate notes of team meetings
     d) all of the above

598. Which of the following statements is not true concerning the
     Bracken Basic Concept Scale?
    *a) is norm-referenced only
     b) is norm-referenced and criterion-referenced
     c) can be used with an associated curriculum package
     d) has colorful artwork

599. The Gesell School Readiness Test
   a) was designed primarily as a test of specific academic skills
   b) is a well constructed, well researched instrument
  *c) indicates whether a child is developmentally young and should be retained
   d) is a group administered instrument

600. The DIAL-3
   a) has good predictive validity
  *b) is primarily a screening device to identify handicapped and gifted preschoolers
   c) a comprehensive test of development
   d) is a time-consuming screening test of development

601. The Boehm Test of Basic Concepts- Revised has an application booklet that assesses concepts used
   a) in mathematics and reading
  *b) in combination, sequences, or in making comparisons
   c) in home , school, and social settings
   d) in making comparisons and analyzing social situations

602. The Behavioral Characteristics Progression
   a) is a norm-referenced instrument
  *b) includes a series of booklets of instructional suggestions
   c) measures a very limited area of functioning
   d) requires a minimal time to administer

603. Which of the following is not true of the Assessment Log?
   a) it is part of the Carolina Curriculum
   b) each child's results are recorded on a Developmental Progress Chart
   c) based on Piaget's theory
  *d) items are scored on a 1 to 5 rating scale

604. The Behavior Characteristics Progression
   a) has no items dealing with academic skills
  *b) groups behaviors into strands
   c) is not appropriate for individuals with severe or profound retardation
   d) cannot he used to assist setting instructional objectives

605. Which of the following is a component of the System to Plan Early Childhood Services?
    a) Developmental
    b) Team
    c) Program
   *d) all of the above

606. Which component of the System To Plan Early Childhood Services allows the comparison of ratings leading to consensus about a child's functioning level across 19 areas?
    a) Developmental
   *b) Team
    c) Program
    d) none of the above

607. The Miller Assessment for Preschoolers is best described as a
    a) comprehensive norm-referenced test
    b) readiness test
   *c) screening test
    d) criterion-referenced test

TRUE-FALSE QUESTIONS

608. The Brigance Inventory of Early Development-Revised (yellow) is quickly administered developmental screening device. F

609. The Vulpe' is a very comprehensive instrument that assesses developmental skills. T

610. The Callier-Azusa includes a coding system for use with individuals with sensory or motor deficits. T

611. The Battelle Developmental Inventory includes guidelines for the administration with children with disabilities. T

612. It is very important that young children be evaluated by a team approach. T

613. The Assessment Log and Developmental Progress Chart is tied into the Carolina Curriculum. T

614. Because of numerous items only portions of criterion-referenced developmental instruments such as the Brigance Inventory are administered. T

615. The Denver II should be used to generate a diagnostic label. F

122

616. The major strength of the Denver II is its strong predictive validity. F

617. The Developmental Profile II is technically inadequate for diagnostic and classification purposes. T

618. The Vulpe' Assessment Battery has a somewhat tedious scoring system. T

619. The Bracken Basic Concept Scale-Revised can be used for norm-referenced or criterion-referenced purposes. T

620. The AGS Early Screening Profile uses information provided by the parent as well as the child. T

621. The DIAL-3 does not measure motor skills. F

622. The Miller Assessment for Preschoolers is a group administered screening instrument. F

623. It may be advantageous to make the testing session more playlike to sustain a preschool child's attention. T

624. The Natural Assessment Model utilizes a very structured environment for assessment purposes. F

625. Play assessment is extremely important when considering the overall developmental status of young children. T

OPEN-ENDED QUESTIONS OR DISCUSSION TOPICS

626. Discuss the benefits of using developmental screening tests In addition, describe any potential problems that could result from the use of these instruments.

627. Is it necessary to administer all of the items of a developmental inventory such as the Vulpe'? Why or why not?

Item #	Page #	Item #	Page #
591.	450	609.	454
592.	449	610.	450,451
593.	417	611.	439
594.	435	612.	417
595.	426	613.	445
596.	414	614.	449
597.	415	615.	426
598.	443	616.	429

599.	444	617.	442
600.	431	618.	453,454
601.	442,443	619.	443
602.	448	620.	421
603.	445,446	621.	430
604.	447	622.	433
605.	418,419	623.	415
606.	418	624.	417,418
607.	434	625.	419.
608.	449		

Chapter 18

Vocational/Transitional Assessment

OVERVIEW AND TEACHING SUGGESTIONS

There has been increased attention on vocational and transitional programming, particularly at the secondary level. This increased emphasis on vocational/transitional programming has lead to a subsequent emphasis on vocational assessment. Whereas past practices in this area have focused on the use of formal instruments, current trends seem to be focused more on informal approaches and are aimed at the development of a comprehensive data base that stretches across a student's school career. This transdisciplinary approach has led to shared responsibilities and cooperative planning and programming that are necessary to achieve successful post-school adjustments for students with disabilities.

Vocational assessment has evolved from and employs the talents of several professional discipline areas. Traditionally, a wide variety of procedures have been utilized during the process of conducting a vocational assessment. This includes the use interviews, rating scales, psychometric testing, work samples, and situational assessment. It has been suggested that a single summative evaluation is insufficient to accurately appraise the interests and attitudes of students with disabilities and that

there should be an increased reliance on the use of work samples,
curriculum-based vocational assessment, and ecological assessment
strategies.   Points to be emphasized in this chapter include the
following:

   *federal mandates impacting on vocational assessment and

    education for students with disabilities

   *the steps in the development of transition plans

   *the role of vocational assessment in the development of

   *transition plans the importance of work samples, curriculum-

    based vocational assessment, and direct observation of

    students on the job.

ACTIVITIES

17-1 JOB SKILL ANALYSIS

Purpose-Provide students with an opportunity to interview
employers to determine job prerequisites and responsibilities.
Description-Have students interview the manager at a local fast
food restaurant (e.g. Burger King).   They should determine what
behaviors/skills are required for an employee to be a) a cook and
b) a cashier.   Students should then identify how thy would
evaluate those skills for a high school student with a mild
disability.   Emphasis should be placed on task analyzing the job
demands.

MULTIPLE CHOICE QUESTIONS

628. Direct observation of activities in the actual work site and
     matching the requirements of the job to the student is a
     process known as
    *a) job match
     b) ecological assessment
     c) work sample
     d) repertoire inventory

629. Curriculum-based vocational assessment (CBVA) was developed
     as a result of which of the following problems?
     a) the use of assessments that measured social behaviors
    *b) assessment information not being used to develop programs
     c) a uniform system of referrals
     d) all or the above

630. Assessment of functional skills in the actual environment
     where those skills are used is an advantage of which of the
     following vocational assessment procedures?
     a) ecological inventory
     b) student repertoire inventory
    *c) both a & b
     d) neither a nor b

631. Which of the following instruments were normed on students
     identified as having learning disabilities and mental
     retardation?
     a) Differential Aptitude Tests
     b) Kuder Occupational Interest Survey
     c) Gordon Occupational Checklists-II
    *d) Reading-Free Vocational Interest Inventory

632. Which of the following instruments provides a Vocational
     Interest Estimate?
    *a) Kuder Occupational Interest Survey
     b) Reading Free Vocational Interest Inventory
     c) Differential Aptitude Tests
     d) all of the above

633. Which of the following instruments includes a supplementary
     test called the Career Interest Inventory?
    *a) Differential Aptitude Tests
     b) Gordon Occupational Checklists-II
     c) Occupational Aptitude and Interest Schedule-2
     d) Reading Free Vocational Interest Inventory-Revised

634. Which statement is not true regarding aptitude and interest
     instruments?
     a) They primarily use a pencil and paper format
    *b) They primarily use an interview format
     c) Some are designed for general education students
     d) Some are designed for special education students

635. Which law expanded the services provided through vocational education assessment to include transition planning and programming?
    a) P.L. 101-476
    b) American with Disabilities Act
    c) P.L. 99-142
   *d) Carl D. Perkins Act

636. The emphasis on career/vocational assessment should substantially _____ as the student enters junior and senior high school, whereas the emphasis on academic assessment should_____.
   *a) increase/decrease
    b) increase/increase
    c) decrease/increase
    d) decrease/decrease

637. Information that may prove to be important during a transition meeting include which of the following?
    a) academic information
    b) social behavior information
    c) psychoeducational information
   *d) all of the above

638. The Wide Range Interest-Opinion Test
    a) can only be administered individually
   *b) does not require reading
    c) has a very small standardization
    d) all of the above

639. Current amendments to IDEA require transition plans to be developed no later than age
    a) 16 years
   *b) 14 years
    c) 12 years
    d) 21 years

640. Gathering vocational-related data concerning a student is known as
   *a) vocational assessment
    b) vocational evaluation
    c) ecological assessment
    d) none of the above

641. Transition plans, as part of the IEP, should be updated at least
     a) every 3 years
     b) every 2 years
    *c) every year
     d) no updates are required

642. Which of the following describes transition plans?
     a) They are broad in scope
     b) They are multi-year in scope
     c) They are included in the IEP
    *d) All of the above

TRUE-FALSE QUESTIONS

643. P.L. 101-476 allowed state education and vocational rehabilitation agencies to receive funding for transition services for students as young as age 10. F

644. Current vocational assessment techniques involve a variety of informal and formal procedures. T

645. Traditional assessment procedures have been abandoned in favor of a transdisciplinary approach to vocational assessment. F

646. The transdisciplinary approach to vocational assessment has led to shared responsibilities and cooperative planning and programming that are necessary for post-secondary success for students with disabilities. T

647. Vocational assessment that relies on a single summative evaluation is probably sufficient for the accurate appraisal of the interests and attitudes of students with disabilities. F

648. There is a trend toward increased reliance on the use of work sample, curriculum-based vocational assessment strategies, and ecological assessment strategies. T

649. Although vocational assessment and vocational evaluation are slightly different, the two terms are often used interchangeably. T

650. The reauthorization of IDEA mandated that all students must have transition plans by age 14. T

651. One potential use for outcome assessment is to provide information for long-term planning and program improvement. T

652. The Americans with Disabilities Act was enacted specifically to increase the likelihood of school to work transitions for students with disabilities. F

653. The Carl D. Perkins Act included transition planning and programming within the context of vocational education. T

654. The more barriers a student faces, the earlier transition planning and programming should begin. T

655. The assessment aspect of of transition planning and programming should begin in a student's last year of public school. F

656. The specific emphasis on career/vocational assessment should increase substantially even before a student enters high school. T

657. Most adult service agencies have sufficient staff to provide transition teams with assessment information and programming recommendations. F

658. Information provided by ratings scales may not provide a complete portrait of a student's aptitudes and abilities. T

659. Activities performed on a work-sample task give the evaluator an opportunity to observe work behavior in the natural work environment. F

660. The Work Adjustment Inventory is a multidimensional instrument that measures work temperament. T

661. Historically, vocational assessments have been conducted with a great deal of collaboration between vocational and special education personnel. F

OPEN-ENDED QUESTIONS OR DISCUSSION TOPICS

662. What are the relative advantages and disadvantages of commercially developed and locally developed work samples?

Item #	Page #	Item #	Page #
628.	473	646.	458
629.	470	647.	459
630.	475	648.	459
631.	486	649.	459
632.	486	650.	461
633.	485	651.	482
634.	484	652.	460
635.	460	653.	460
636.	463	654.	460
637.	462	655.	461,462
638.	488	656.	462
639.	461	657.	462
640.	459	658.	464
641.	465	659.	468
642.	463,465	660.	468
643.	460	661.	484
644.	459	662.	470
645.	458		

NOTES

NOTES

NOTES

NOTES

NOTES